The Record of Tung-shan

KURODA INSTITUTE
Classics in East Asian Buddhism

The Record of Tung-shan

Translated by

WILLIAM F. POWELL

UNIVERSITY OF HAWAII PRESS

Honolulu

The Kuroda Institute for the Study of Buddhism and Human Values is a non-profit, educational corporation, founded in 1976. One of its primary objectives is to promote scholarship on Buddhism in its historical, philosophical, and cultural ramifications. The Institute thus attempts to serve the scholarly community by providing a forum in which scholars can gather at conferences and colloquia. To date, the Institute has sponsored six conferences in the area of Buddhist Studies, and volumes resulting from these conferences are published in the Institute's Studies in East Asian Buddhism series. To complement these scholarly studies, the Institute will also make available reliable translations of some of the major classics of East Asian Buddhism in the present series.

Library of Congress Cataloging-in-Publication Data

Liang-chieh, 807–869.
  The record of Tung-shan.

  (Classics in East Asian Buddhism)
  Translation of: Tung-shan Wu-pen-ch'an-shih yü lu.
  Bibliography: p.
  1. Zen Buddhism—Early works to 1800. I. Powell, William F., 1940–   . II. Title. III. Series.
  BQ9449.L524T8613   1986   294.3'927   86–4305
  ISBN 0–8248–1070–8

Calligraphy by
Suigan Yogo Rōshi
of Daiyūzan Saijōji

Contents

Foreword

Tung-shan Liang-chieh was intimate with the source of all categories, and thus he could present their unity and their particular virtues with vivid clarity:

A monk asked, "how does one escape hot and cold?"

"Why not go where it is neither hot nor cold?" said the Master.

"What sort of place is neither hot nor cold?" asked the monk.

"When it's cold you freeze to death; when it's hot you swelter to death."

The reason you die with the cold is that you dwell where there is neither cold nor heat. The reason you die with the birdsong is that you dwell where there is neither sound nor silence.

Dying with the cold or the birdsong is the great life of cold or the birdsong. The great life of standing up and sitting down rests firmly on the experience of body and mind falling away.

Tung-shan is renouned as the founder of the sect we know today as Sōtō Zen Buddhism, and as the author of the poetical treatise, "The Five Ranks," studies by all Zen students regardless of sect. His great achievements arise from hearing vividly with his eyes the sermons of birds and trees, and from his cultivation of that realization in tireless personal practice and teaching.

William Powell has enhanced the understanding of the Buddha Dharma for Western readers with his exemplary translation and study of Tung-shan's great life. I am most thankful to him and to all others who made this publication possible.

Robert Aitken
Koko An Zendō
Honolulu

Preface

In twenty out of the ninety-five chapters that compose the *Shōbōgenzō*, the Zen master Dōgen quotes extensively from Tung-shan's public addresses, dialogues, Dharma lectures, and random sayings. He also shows the high esteem in which he held Tung-shan by referring to him using his honorific title and posthumous name, "The Eminent Monk, Wu-pen of Tung-shan." It is evident that Dōgen studied the teachings of Tung-shan and his lineage with great devotion. That Tung-shan, in his role as founder of Chinese Ts'ao-tung Ch'an, had established the foundation for a unique way of approaching Buddhism earned Dogen's greatest respect.

To Dōgen, for whom "leaving home to practice the Way" had the greatest significance in the study of the Buddha Way, Tung-shan's life became a model. According to accounts of Tung-shan's life, he suffered the sad fate of "not having anyone to rely on, his father having died, his mother grown old, and his brothers become cold and distant." It was recorded that "his mother did not have the heart to reject her child (Tung-shan), but it was the child's intention to abandon her." However, Tung-shan had the firm conviction that, "in order to cut off the desirous river of life and death and to cross the bitter sea of defilements, nothing is comparable to the merit of leaving home [to become a monk]." This corresponds to Dōgen's own single-minded resolve to leave home to practice the Way. Because of this he never lapsed in his reverence for the example Tung-shan had set.

Although there have been numerous editions of this discourse record, generally abbreviated as *The Record of Tung-shan,* the one with the widest popularity in Japan has been the Chinese Ming edition obtained by Gimoku Genkai, who re-edited and published it with his own epilogue in 1739. Little is known about Genkai, even the date of his death being uncertain, but his epilogue, "from the brush of the Japanese *śramaṇa,* Genkai, of Zuiryu Monastery in Utaura," gives some indication of who he was. Zuiryu Monastery is the present Rinsen Temple of Zuiryusan, also known as Hakkarin, located at Nishinomachi, Hatayashiki of Wakayama City. Although Genkai is regarded as being in the lineage of Jirin Genshi (d. 1764), a member of the ninth generation of Rinsen Temple, and also in the thirty-seventh generation of Daijo Temple in Ishi-kawa-ken, Genkai himself is not listed in the generational records of Rinsen Temple. In any case, Genkai wholeheartedly applied himself to the study of *The Record of Tung-shan*. We can be extremely grateful for the effort he expended in compiling a register of the twenty-seven members of Tung-shan's Dharma lineage, and for his critical textual analysis of more than sixteen capping phrases.

The Kuroda Institute for the Study of Buddhism and Human Values, under the leadership of Hakuyu Maezumi Roshi, has made a great contribution to the propagation of True Dharma Zen through their publication of this English translation of *The Record of Tung-shan*. I hope for its success. They have published a relatively large number of translations of the classics of the Buddhas and Patriarchs. Such practice of the Way manifests their deep respect.

The many poems and *gāthās* in the text, such as "The Jewel Mirror *Samādhi*," "The Five Ranks," and "Lords and Vassals," all of which concern the Five Ranks doctrine, are a uniquely Eastern form of poetic expression. It must not have been easy to translate them. I offer this preface, then, in the hope that the essence of the teaching will be grasped and the benefits of the Dharma may be made widely accessible.

Shuyu Sakurai
President
Komazawa University
Japan

Abbreviations

CTL   *Ching-te ch'uan-teng lu (The Transmission of the Lamp Compiled During the Ching-te Era)*

T.   *Taishō shinshū daizōkyō*

TSL   *Jui-chou Tung-shan Liang-chieh ch'an-shih yü-lu (The Record of Tung-shan)*

TTC   *Tsu-t'ang chi (The Collection from the Patriarchal Hall)*

WCYL   *Wu-chia yü-lu (Discourse Records of the Five Houses)*

Z.   *Dainihon zokuzōkyō*

Introduction

The period from 755 to 907, although traditionally regarded as the waning years of the T'ang Dynasty, was a period of flourishing development for Ch'an Buddhism. The An Lu-shan rebellion of 755, from which the dynasty had great difficulty recovering, marked the beginning of what traditional histories have regarded as the declining years of the T'ang. This decline ended with the establishment of the Liang Dynasty in 907. During this period, Chinese Buddhism underwent one of its periodic persecutions, one from which much of the Buddhist establishment never fully recovered. Emperor Wu Tsung's suppression of Buddhism in 845 marked the end of many of the more traditional and scholastic Buddhist movements in China. Yet it was precisely during this period that Ch'an Buddhists were in the midst of one of their most creative and formative phases, one that was to have major influence on all later Ch'an Buddhism, not only in China, but also in Korea, Japan, and in recent times even America and Europe. While acknowledging such earlier figures as Bodhidharma and Hui-neng, almost all Ch'an lineages from the end of the T'ang trace their doctrinal and institutional origins to various masters of this period.

This era stands between two other distinct periods in the development of Ch'an Buddhism. What might be termed the early period begins around the sixth or seventh century, shortly after Bodhidharma is said to have arrived in China. It continues through the middle of the eighth century, when the Sixth Patriarch, Hui-neng, and his immediate disciples, particularly Shen-hui, were active. During this period Ch'an Buddhists were becoming conscious of themselves as a distinct tradition within Buddhism and were establishing their legitimacy in the eyes of Chinese society. The issues with which they were concerned, at least toward the end of the early period, are probably those presented in the *Platform Sutra of the Sixth Patriarch*. Not only does this document express the thought of what has come to be known as the "Southern Lineage," but, as recent research is beginning to show, it incorporates much of the thought of the "Northern Lineage" as well.[1] The late period of Ch'an development begins in the middle of the eleventh century with the systemization of Ch'an into the "Five Houses" *(Wu-chia)* and continues sporadically until the present.

The impression one gets from the various accounts of the Ch'an Buddhism of the middle period is of an elaborate network of masters, each transmitting his own creative understanding of Buddhism to numerous followers who wandered from master to master. Questions of lineage legitimacy, which characterized the early period, were no longer in evidence. The narrowing of the various lineages to five "houses," with their characteristic teachings or styles, had yet to occur. Most of the activity in the middle period was concentrated south of the Yangtse River, principally in an area west of Lake Po-yang in modern Kiangsi Province (see map, p. 22). In and around this area, known during the Sui and T'ang dynasties as Hung-chou, were located the centers of Ma-tsu (709–788), Pai-chang (720–814), Huang-po (d. 850), Tung-shan (807–869), Yün-chü (835?–902), Ts'ao-shan (840–901), and Yang-shan (807–883). Slightly farther west of this area in modern Hunan were located the centers of Yün-yen (d. 850) and Kuei-shan (771–853). To the east in modern Fukien was the center of Hsüeh-feng(822–908). Lin-chi (d. 866), who eventually established his center far to the north, began his career in Hung-chou under Huang-p'o. All of these well-known masters were considered distinctly individualistic in their teaching styles and personalities. However, the fact that they were all contemporaries or near contemporaries, that their centers, except for Lin-chi's, were located in close proximity to one another, and that their students were in the habit of regularly visiting the other masters in the region gave to the Ch'an of this period a coherence and momentum that undoubtedly contributed to the significant later influence of this group of masters.

Liang-chieh of Tung-shan is one of the many masters who contributed to the creative energy of this flourishing middle period of Ch'an history. Unfortunately, biographical information on Tung-shan, as for most of the Ch'an figures of this period, is extremely sparse, being limited to a few pieces of mundane information such as dates, family name, and birthplace. In fact, the lack of reliable information on the figures of the middle period is an issue of some significance. Perhaps, as Paul Demiéville suggests, such information existed but was destroyed by the Buddhist persecution of 845.[2] Or possibly there were internal reasons, attitudes within Ch'an itself, that mitigated against the making or preservation of records.

According to the data we do have, Tung-shan was born in 807 in Kuei-chi, a town in southeastern Shao-hsing district of Chekiang Province, an area rich in legend and religious tradition. The mountain of Kuei-chi was popularly believed to be the site of the tomb of Yü, the legendary first ruler of the semi-historical Hsia Dynasty (2183–1752 B.C.E.). Not far to the southeast is Mt. T'ien-t'ai, the great Buddhist center founded by Chih-i (538–597). This mountain is also associated with the eccentric Ch'an poet of the T'ang dynasty Han-shan. To the west is Mt. Wu-hsieh, where Tung-shan took his monastic vows. Due east is Mt. T'ai-pai, the site of T'ien-t'ung Temple, to which the great Japanese monk Dōgen (1200–1253) came in the thirteenth century to study the teaching of Tung-shan under Ju-ching (1163–1228).

Tung-shan was a contemporary of Lin-chi (d. 866), the founder of another major Ch'an lineage. Like Lin-chi, Tung-shan spent much of his early life visiting Ch'an masters and recluses in the Hung-chou region. This must have been about the time of the great Buddhist suppression of 845, but if this momentous event had any effect on Tung-shan, there is no indication in any of the records. He eventually established his own center on "Cave Mountain" *(tung-shan)* in Hung-chou (modern Nanchang hsien in the province of Kiangsi), where, among his disciples, the two most notable were Yün-chü (835?–902) and Ts'ao-shan (840–901). Yün-chü's branch of Tung-shan's lineage survived in China until the seventeenth century and was carried to Japan by Dōgen in the thirteenth, where it continues to the present as the Sōtō Zen sect. Ironically, Ts'ao-shan's branch did not survive his immediate disciples, but because he is regarded as having been personally entrusted by Tung-shan with, among other teachings, the famous Five Ranks doctrine, he continues to be held in high regard by Buddhists of various lineages. Tung-shan died in 869.

The Nature of the Text

The text for *The Record of Tung-shan* translated here occurs as an independent work in the *Taishō* Buddhist Canon (T.1986) but originated as part of a collection of discourse records, *The Records of the Five Houses (Wu-chia yü-lu)*, compiled in 1632. This work also contains the discourse records of Lin-chi, Yün-men, Fa-yen, Kuei-shan, Yang-shan, and Ts'ao-shan. It is significant that the discourse record for Tung-shan included in this collection was compiled not by a member of Tung-shan's own lineage, but by members of Lin-chi's lineage, principally Yü-feng Yüan-hsin (1571–1647). This work, Tung-shan's earliest extant discourse record, does not appear until eight hundred years after his death.

By way of perspective, we today are removed from the compilers of this text by only half as many years as they were from Tung-shan. In contrast, the discourse record of Tung-shan's contemporary Lin-chi was completed five hundred years earlier, in 1120. If it were not for the existence of earlier collections of Tung-shan anecdotes, we might reasonably question the authenticity of a record of discourse published so long after the events it purports to describe.

The two most important earlier works which include much of the material contained in *The Record of Tung-shan* are *The Collection from the Patriarchal Hall (Tsu-t'ang chi)*, completed in 952, and *The Transmission of the Lamp Compiled During the Ching-te Era (Ching-te ch'uan-teng lu)*, completed in 1004. These two texts belong to a separate genre of anecdote collections known as "lamp records" *(teng-lu)*. Their general content is the same as the discourse records, but the organizing principle is distinctly different. In terms of lineage, lamp records are comprehensive rather than exclusive. Most of the known Ch'an lineages are represented, and the records of numerous disciples of each teacher are included. The lamp records are repositories of the composite heritage of the middle period; their inclusiveness gives support to Mahāyāna Buddhism's claim that many individuals are capable of enlightenment, not just one in each generation. Thus the lamp records counter the view given in many earlier Ch'an texts (e.g., the *Pao-lin chuan*) of a somewhat elitist, one-to-one transmission, master to disciple, stretching back in a single tenuous, but unbroken line to Shakyamuni Buddha. The structure of the lamp records suggests a new awareness and appreciation of the collective experience of Ch'an.

The Collection from the Patriarchal Hall appeared at the very end of the middle period of Ch'an, a time when the unity of the T'ang had disintegrated into rapidly changing, unstable dynasties and the foreign occupation of the North. The collection was compiled by Ching-hsiu Wen-teng (no dates) and two of his disciples, known only as Ching and Yün. Ching-hsiu was a disciple of Hsüeh-feng, whose monastery was located in south China near the thriving port city of Ch'üan-chou. After the fall of the T'ang this region become the kingdom of Min, one of ten kingdoms established in the South. Min, in contrast to much of the rest of China, enjoyed considerable peace and stability, thus becoming a refuge for, among others, monks fleeing the insecurity of the North. Hsüeh-feng is said to have attracted 1,700 students and disciples from all over China and from various lineages. In such an eclectic environment and at that particular time in Chinese history, the many anecdotes the various monks had brought with them would naturally have become topics for discussion and comment. As a result, Ching and Yün were provided with a ready supply of lore from which to compile their collection. The text consists of twenty chapters and contains the records of 257 figures.

Although *The Collection from the Patriarchal Hall* contains the earliest collection of Tung-shan anecdotes, it was probably not available to the editors of our text. The work appears to have been forgotten and lost from the middle of the thirteenth century to the twentieth century. Perhaps it was superseded by *The Transmission of the Lamp,* which had been included by imperial command in the main body of the Sung printing of the Buddhist Canon. *The Collection from the Patriarchal Hall* was rediscovered in Korea in 1926 by two Japanese scholars, Sekino Tadashi and Ono Genmyō, in 1926 along with fourteen other extra-canonical works among the wood blocks of the Korean Buddhist Canon stored at Haein-sa Monastery. A study of the contents of this early lamp history confirms the late tenth-century existence of many of the anecdotes included in our sixteenth-century text.

The Transmission of the Lamp, though of the same lamp record genre and compiled only fifty-two years later, differs from *The Collection from the Patriarchal Hall* in two important respects: the number of figures was greatly expanded, and the style is far more literary. *The Transmission of the Lamp,* compiled by Yung-an Tao-yüan (no dates), a member of the Fa-yen lineage, contains the records of 1,701 figures, 1,444 more than in *The Collection from the Patriarchal Hall.* The literary, almost classical style of *The Transmission of the Lamp* contrasts sharply with the rustic, colloquial style of the earlier text and thus reads less like a record of authentic discourse. The Sung editors of *The Transmission of the Lamp* were apparently striving to appeal to a more literate and sophisticated audience. This literary style is also characteristic of *The Record of Tung-shan,* which is not suprising, since the editors of the later text would certainly have had *The Transmission of the Lamp* as one of their primary sources.

The discourse record *(yü-lu)* genre, of which our text is an example, first appeared at about the same time as the lamp records, i.e., at the beginning of the Sung Dynasty. In many ways, this genre reflects developments in the Ch'an of this late period more accurately than the lamp records. Having survived the 845 persecution and the collapse of the T'ang Dynasty, Ch'an began to take on the characteristics of an established institution in the Sung. The amorphous energy of its middle period gave way to system and order. For example, the "Five Houses"—the Kuei-yang, Lin-chi, Ts'ao-tung, Yün-men, and Fa-yen—emerged as recognized Ch'an institutions out of the miscellany of masters and teachings of the T'ang. In Sung Ch'an literature we see an attempt on the part of some to identify the "house style" *(chia-feng)* of these five sublineages. What probably began as mere tendencies or functions of personality in the early masters and their immediate disciples took on, when viewed in retrospect, greater form and reality in the Sung editors' eyes. The discourse records bring together in one place material on individual masters, material that previously had been scattered throughout various works and even within a single work. In the lamp records the anecdotes involving a particular figure are usually found not just in his own section, but also in that of his master, the various other masters he may have visited, and his students. Thus the discourse records focus attention on individual masters rather than on the collective heritage.

These records are not biographies in the traditional sense, since they generally provide little more concrete information than a figure's birthplace and family name. All else tends to be anecdotal snatches of conversation derived primarily from lineage histories and lamp records. Though not biographical, discourse records do appear to convey a sense of the personalities and, by extension, the "house style" of the figures who composed a particular lineage. In fact, they might be described as "word portraits" of the patriarchs, comparable to the actual portraits traditionally made of a master by his designated successor (see *TSL* 9). Without setting forth a systematic teaching, the compilers of the discourse records may have been attempting to preserve and transmit through the characters of individual masters, what they perceived to be the style of particular houses. If this was indeed the case, the text was probably intended to be read as a whole, rather than as a collection of discrete incidents, since style or personality can only emerge from a sense of the whole.

The lamp and discourse records should be clearly distinguished from the *kung-an* (Jap., *koan*) collections, which are better known in the West but are an entirely separate genre of Ch'an literature. The *kung-an* collections, which began to appear in the Sung Dynasty, are anthologies of anecdotes, called "cases," that for one reason or another had come to be considered useful devices in inducing some form of enlightenment in aspiring students. To each of the anecdotes is generally added one or more commentaries. These collections were apparently intended to function as courses of study, or possibly "teacher manuals," though it is still unclear exactly how they were used during this early period. Although they draw on the same pool of anecdotes as the other genres discussed earlier, the structure of the texts does not provide any sense of lineage, house style, individual masters, or collective Ch'an experience. Instead, the structure tends to focus attention on individual "cases." Thus these collections were a new and unique adaption of the anecdote to a particular end. To avoid confusion, "anecdote" has been used here in place of the familiar *koan* or its translation, "case."

In addition to structural differences, *The Record of Tung-shan* includes material not found in the lamp records. In fact, it is about a third longer than the Tung-shan sections in either *The Collection from the Patriarchal Hall* or *The Transmission of the Lamp*. Some of this increase may be accounted for by the inclusion of much verse or *gāthā,* as it was known in Buddhist terms, that had not been a part of the earlier narrative but could be found in other relatively early documents. The discourse record also contains anecdotes from the sections of other figures in the lamp records that included Tung-shan as a secondary participant. This still leaves a small number of anecdotes for which we have no earlier record. It is, of course, possible that we have simply lost an earlier record of these "new" anecdotes, but it seems more likely that, over the period of eight hundred years, material from external sources has crept in. There is also an occasional variation or embellishment in a particular anecdote, but these do not appear to be significant.

Perhaps the most important difference is that of literary style, which, as indicated earlier, is also one of the major differences between the two lamp records. Of course, minor changes in content may have been made in the process of polishing the anecdotes; i.e., what may have been viewed as mere improvements in style or language might, in fact, have significantly altered the substance. If nothing else, the tone must have been affected. Changing T'ang vernacular into Sung literary language might be compared to translating New York City street slang into Oxford English.

It should now be obvious, based on a consideration of the sources on Tung-shan and the various genres they represent, that our present text cannot be taken with certainty as an accurate representation of the eighth-century Ch'an master. For one thing, that representation is based on late-period texts of a middle-period figure. The text that might correspond most closely to a middle-period perspective is *The Collection from the Patriarchal Hall,* but *The Record of Tung-shan* is a distinct departure from that perspective both in format and in style. In fact, even *The Collection from the Patriarchal Hall* cannot have escaped some interpolation, since it was compiled eighty years after Tung-shan's death and is only as accurate as the perceptions and memories of its transmitters. Conceivably some incidents, the import of which Tung-shan may have regarded as central to his teaching, were neglected and forgotten by certain disciples somewhere in the line of transmission because they failed to grasp their significance. Conversely, other less important incidents may have been misunderstood and overvalued and, as a result, incorporated into the narrative.

Thus the actual person and teachings of Tung-shan must remain as shadows behind the work we are considering here. The various texts we have considered represent a series of successive impressions that were gradually polished and modified, influenced no doubt by the concerns of the compilers' own times. It is as though Tung-shan were a drop of water that, on striking a pond, was totally swallowed up, leaving only a set of concentric ripples. Even literary records are subject to impermanence and conditioned co-arising. *The Record of Tung-shan*, then, represents a crystalization in one particular time and place, seventeenth-century central China, of a process that an apparently obscure man set in motion eight hundred years earlier. Whether or not it is historically accurate, the image of Tung-shan and his lineage presented here is the one that later Buddhists were given, and the one that has influenced generations of Ch'an students. It is impossible to say exactly how early that image emerged, but its main outlines were probably present by mid-Sung.

Doctrinal Origins of the Discourse Record

One of the problems faced by the reader of the discourse records is that they do not present teachings or ideas that one commonly associates with earlier Buddhist literature, not to mention religious literature in general. The anecdotes are not the transparant parables of the Christian Bible or early Buddhist sutras, nor are they moralistic or normative vignettes in the tradition of the Confucian *Analects*. The very structure of the anecdotes clearly distinguishes them from the systematic and analytical treatises that occupied the energies of many earlier Buddhist exegetes and teachers, such as Seng-chao (374–414), Chih-i (538–597), or Fa-tsang (643–712). But this is only to be expected from a tradition that characterizes itself as a "teaching outside words." Given Ch'an's very self-conscious proclamation of freedom from words, however, how are we to account for and understand such Ch'an literary documents as the discourse records? Where the tradition itself falls silent, we must look elsewhere.

One way to understand the discourse records, and *The Record of Tung-shan* in particular, is through an awareness of certain seminal ideas and doctrines in the development of Chinese Buddhist thought through the ninth century. Principal among these were the Perfection of Wisdom

(Prajñāpāramitā) doctrine of emptiness *(śūnyatā)*, the Hua-yen doctrine of the mutual interpenetration of principle and phenomena, and the Ch'an teaching of the "mirrorlike mind." In tracing the evolution of Chinese Buddhist thinking, we describe a trajectory that may offer some clues about the direction of that thought once the tradition ceased to be explicit about itself.

One of the earliest systems of Buddhist thought to attract attention in China was the Perfection of Wisdom. The principal source of interpretation of this body of Buddhist thought in China was a commentary attributed to Nāgārjuna, the *Ta-chih-tu lun*, which was translated by Kumārajīva in the late forth century. Emptiness was understood in this tradition, in one sense, as the perception of reality that resulted from a deconstruction of the conceptual[3] and verbal framework by which other Buddhists had sought to rationalize Buddhist teaching. The earlier Buddhist tradition had produced the Abhidharma, an analysis of reality into discrete elements known as dharmas. This approach entailed a relatively complex conceptual framework by which an attempt was made to account conceptually for such Buddhist doctrines as the distinction between defiled existence in the mundane world (samsara) and the purified state of cessation (nirvana). Nāgārjuna sought to demonstrate the fallacy of all such dichotomizing conceptualization without, in the process, substituting a new concept of reality in the resultant void. Thus language and reason were used in Perfection of Wisdom thought not to generate concepts, but as an antidote to conceptualization. When the *Diamond Sutra,* a short Perfection of Wisdom text, says, "One should produce a thought that is nowhere supported by anything," it calls for speech that neither depends on concepts nor results in them. This line from the *Diamond Sutra* was said to have first enlightened Hui-neng, the Sixth Chinese Ch'an Patriarch. Could this line be expressing, in seminal form, the Ch'an idea of "a teaching outside words," where "words" are thoughts supported by concepts, and "teaching" is, among other things, the use of language free from conceptualization? Nāgārjuna's use of language to deconstruct seems to be a use of language that depends on nothing, in the sense of not arising out of an opposing conceptual system.

The Perfection of Wisdom suggests at least two attitudes relevant to the discourse records. It discredits the language of conceptualization, and it undermines distinctions made between samsara and nirvana, ignorance and enlightenment, and phenomenal and ultimate reality. Again, in the *Diamond Sutra* we read, "Form is not different from emptiness; emptiness is not different from form." In addition, Nāgārjuna demonstrates a performative use of language, in contrast to a merely informative use. In the discourse records, language is rarely used to inform; where doctrines are mentioned, it is usually for the purpose not of elucidating them, but of discrediting all such attempts. Language is used not for its ability to build concepts, but for its affective impact on the hearer or reader. The acumen of much of the language used in these texts belies the conclusion that such an anti-conceptual religious tradition would deteriorate into some form of know-nothing piety. And, in denying the dichotomy between samsara and nirvana, the Perfection of Wisdom provided the theoretical foundation for seeing ultimate reality as totally present in this-worldly, mundane activity.

To deny the duality of samsara and nirvana, as the Perfection of Wisdom does, or to demonstrate logically the error of dichotomizing conceptualization, as Nāgārjuna does, is not to address the question of the relationship between samsara and nirvana—or, in more philosophical terms, between phenomenal and ultimate reality. Some might be disabused of their concepts or views by Nāgārjuna's dialectic and thereby glimpse emptiness; others, through meditation, might attain a similar experience; but all continue to exist and function in the world of phenomena. What, then, is the relationship between these two realms? It was partly in response to this question that the Chinese Hua-yen master Fa-tsang developed his teaching on the mutual interpenetration of principle *(li)* and phenomena *(shih)*. On the one hand, according to this teaching, principle and phenomena can be thought of as quite distinct from each other. The experience of emptiness as it occurs in some forms of meditation, for example, is markedly different, on the surface at least, from worldly activity such as carrying wood. On the other hand, according to Fa-tsang, each implies the other by means of mutual interpenetration. To illustrate this, he cited the example of the golden lion, in which the relationship of the gold to the lion's form was analogous to the relationship between principle and phenomena. The gold always exists in some form, whether or not it is in such a familiar form as a lion. Similarly, the lion form is nonexistent apart from the gold. Thus they mutually interpenetrate.

Whereas Nāgārjuna and his Chinese interpreters tend to leave off at a highly intellectual, logically induced experience of emptiness, the Hua-yen masters emphasized the relationship of emptiness to form and attempted to describe the dynamics of that relationship. Those dynamics were elaborated by Ch'eng-kuan (738–839) in his teachings on the "Fourfold *Dharmadhatu*," where experience was categorized into four modes: (1) the world of phenomena, (2) the world of principle, (3) the world of perfectly interpenetrating phenomena and principle, and (4) the world of perfectly interpenetrating phenomena and phenomena. This approach contained two important implications for the discourse records: the recognition of a plurality of modes for experiencing reality and a theoretical basis for greater attention to the phenomenal world.

The willingness to accept various modes of experience as valid manifestations of reality or the *dharmadhatu* meant that one need not limit Buddhist practices to those that lead to an experience of reality as unadulterated emptiness. Enlightenment need not be sought in an experience of emptiness or purified consciousness, such as that suggested in the second Hua-yen category; it could also reveal itself through any of the other three modes of experience. We see a similar understanding and approach in Lin-chi's "Four Classifications" *(ssu-liao-chien),*[4] as well as in Tung-shan's "Five Ranks" *(wu-wei;* see *TSL* 114, 115, 116, 117). Both present modes of experiencing in terms of the relationship between ultimate and apparent reality. The following passage from the *Heart Sutra* might also be interpreted in a similar manner:

> Form is emptiness,
> Emptiness is form;
> Form is not different from emptiness,
> Emptiness is not different from form.

The Five Ranks of Tung-shan are (1) phenomena within the real *(cheng chung p'ien),* (2) the real within phenomena *(p'ien chung cheng),* (3) coming from within the real *(cheng chung lai),* (4) going within together *(chien chung chih),* and (5) arriving within together *(chien chung tao).* Though the word "rank" has been used, there is no indication in Tung-shan that these are any more than unprioritized modes of experience. In other words, they do not necessarily represent a kind of "pilgrim's progress," in which one begins with the first rank and moves systematically to the fifth. The first rank suggests an experience of reality in which "form is emptiness." According to the Perfection of Wisdom, all phenomena, when correctly understood, are no more than the ultimate truth of emptiness. Such an experience of reality might, for example, result from the conceptual reductionism taught by Nāgārjuna. The second rank presents the experience from the opposite perspective, i.e., that the truth of emptiness can be manifested in phenomenal events: "Emptiness is form." Thus ultimate reality may be revealed to the mind's eye in concrete phenomena. Metaphor and poetry are ideally suited to function in this way, and it is this capacity of poetry that may account for its frequent use in Ch'an literature. In *The Record of Tung-shan,* metaphor and poetry are particulary common. The third rank returns the focus to the real, or emptiness. This suggests the experience of reality that results from an absorption in emptiness, as in meditation. In the fourth rank, attention is redirected to phenomena, where phenomena are totally identified with emptiness. Phenomena, things, when experienced in a particular frame of mind, are not merely metaphorical representions of the ultimate; they are directly experienced as the ultimate. Thus, the most mundane of daily activities, such as washing one's bowls, need not point to anything outside of itself when it is experienced as emptiness: "Emptiness is not different from form." The fifth rank seems to be an attempt to account for a completely harmonious experience of reality that transcends the previous four and in which neither form nor emptiness is emphasized, though both are fully present. Thus it can be seen that Ch'an thought was closely related to the Hua-yen categorization of the modes of interaction between principle and phenomena.

Not only did Hua-yen philosophy offer several different modes of experiencing reality, but it also provided an explicit theoretical foundation for seeking enlightenment amidst mundane phenomena. Of the Hua-yen categories, the first, the world of phenomena, and the third, the world of the interpenetration of principle and phenomena, appear to be of particular relevance to middle-period Ch'an and the discourse records. These two categories provide an ingenious solution to the problem of using language to talk about ultimate reality without necessarily falling into the trap of conceptualizing it. Instead of talking about emptiness in abstract, analytical terms, as was common in much Buddhist literature, one could approach it in concrete, phenomenal terms, the ordinary language of everyday events. If principle was totally interfused with phenomena, then any act, no matter how mundane, could manifest principle. For example, the National Teacher Hui-chung in *TSL* 3 describes the mind of the ancient Buddhas as "wall and tile rubble." This statement, incidentally, is reminiscent of an attitude found in Chinese literature that predates the arrival of Buddhism in China. In the *Chuang Tzu,* we find the Tao described as existing in crickets, grasses, tiles and even shit and piss.[5] Thus the theoretical basis for discovering the ultimate in phenomena, however humble or mundane, is not only quite explicit in Hua-yen thought, but also had precedent in the Chinese philosophical-literary tradition.

The final indication of the direction of Chinese Buddhist thought that we will mention here is the manner in which the Ch'an simile of the mirrorlike mind was being used around the end of the eighth century, approximately at the transition point between the early and middle periods of Ch'an development. The simile was used in at least two different senses. It often implied the inherently pure mind that existed beneath what for most beings is the disturbed surface of consciousness. Most Chinese Buddhist thinkers held that that pure mind existed in all beings and could no more be defiled than a mirror could be defiled by the images reflected on its surface. This particular attitude was probably shared by most early eighth-century Ch'an Buddhists. Note that this is not the gradualistic sense of the mirror-mind, which implied the need for constant wiping—a sense attributed by the *Platform Sutra,* perhaps unjustly, to Shen-hsiu.[6] The other use of the simile was as the mind that constantly functions, spontaneously and accurately, in the midst of the phenomenal world. Like a mirror it immediately reflects exactly what is placed before it. This was the sense, more dynamic than the first, that came to predominate in eighth- and ninth-century Ch'an. Not that the earlier attitude was denied—there was merely a shift in emphasis.

If this latter sense was indeed the one held by most Ch'an Buddhists, then they might reasonably expect to find reality most clearly manifested in the words and deeds of their enlightened masters. This, in fact, seems to be what Ma-tsu is implying in his statement, "This very mind is the Buddha Mind." Since the enlightened mind, like a mirror, is constantly reflecting and responding spontaneously to reality, all its functions are potentially instructive. The patriarchs of Ch'an need only carry out their routine activities or speak in everyday terms to manifest their pure minds, and thus ultimate reality itself. In this view, to analyze that reality would be not only useless, but also counterproductive. The discourse records appear to be the fruit of these attitudes.

Themes and Style

Although it would be inadvisable, given the nature of the discourse records, to attempt a systematic interpretation of *The Record of Tung-shan,* we can at least identify several principal themes, as well as certain stylistic tendencies, that suggest the attitudes of the compilers. A discussion of these themes and tendencies is intended to suggest how the text goes about transmitting its meaning, rather than what the text means.

A theme that occurs throughout Ch'an discourse records is the failure, and even the counterproductivity, of the exegetical approach to sutra commentary and Buddhist texts. Exegetes and pedants are frequently held up for ridicule. *The Record of Tung-shan* does not depart from this tradition. Where Nāgārjuna carefully dismantles the reasoning of doctrinal theorists, the discourse records caricature them. No attempt is made to discredit them by means of logic. Tung-shan generally does the job by badgering them with questions they are unable to answer. In one short exchange, Tung-shan asks an official who intended to write a commentary on the *Inscription on Believing in Mind (Hsin hsin ming)*, a poem attributed to the Third Ch'an Patriarch, the meaning of the line "As soon as there is assertion and denial, the mind is lost in confusion." The official makes no answer, and a note suggests that the official decided not to write the commentary after all (*TSL* 24). A variation on this theme occurs when a student asks Tung-shan a question calling for explanation. In this case Tung-shan generally either refuses to answer the question or responds in some unexpected manner. For example, in *TSL* 82 a monk asks Tung-shan the meaning of a particular couplet from a Ch'an poem. Tung-shan merely joins his palms and raises them above his head. Whatever the significance of this act, it is clearly not an explanation.

Nonetheless, Tung-shan is not always adverse to commenting on sutras or poetry. When asked the meaning of the line "Amidst the darkling, darken again" in *TSL* 97, he replies with a simile: "It's like a dead person's tongue." In the several other instances in the text when he does reply to such questions, it is also by means of simile. Apparently, some forms of commentary are acceptable. As indicated earlier, Tung-shan suggested the possibility of revealing the ultimate through phenomena in the second of his Five Ranks. Similes are ideally suited for this purpose. Also, in *TSL* 117 Tung-shan is quite explicit about the kind of language that is unacceptable. In discussing three types of defilement present in the world, he identifies one as "defiled language." This defilement, says Tung-shan, is "mastering trivia and losing sight of the essential. The result is that the potential for enlightenment is thoroughly obscured." This suggests the excessively analytical use of language to which pedants are prone. Thus Tung-shan does not seem to be rejecting all uses of language to talk about the ultimate, only those that are overly pedantic and analytical.

Another conspicuous theme, important not only in Ch'an, but in other schools of Mahāyāna Buddhism as well, is the possession of Buddha Nature by all beings, animate as well as inanimate. At the beginning of the fifth century, the monk Tao-sheng had asserted that all sentient beings, even *icchantikas,* the incorrigibles of traditional Buddhism, possessed Buddha Nature and were thus capable of attaining the way. This assertion stirred a storm of controversy but was eventually born out by the newly arrived Dharmakṣema translation of the *Nirvāṇa Sūtra,* made in 421. Yün-chü, Tung-shan's disciple, appears to echo that early debate in *TSL* 47, where he ironically describes the *icchantika's* behavior as filial. In the eighth century, Chan-jan, the ninth patriarch of the T'ien-t'ai School, argued that Buddha Nature extended even to nonsentient beings by pointing out that to distinguish between animate and inanimate beings in the question of Buddha Nature was to fall into a false dualism. If, as the T'ien-t'ai maintained, all things are manifestations of the One Mind, then just as all sentient beings possessed Buddha Nature, mountains and rivers must also possess Buddha Nature.[7] This theme is introduced early in *The Record of Tung-shan* and appears to have been the topic that led Tung-shan to his master, Yün-yen. In pursuing the question of how it is possible for nonsentient beings to expound the Dharma, T'ung-shan goes first to Kuei-shan, who in turn directs him to Yün-yen. Yün-yen's response to this question obviously impresses Tung-shan, since he remains as Yün-yen's disciple (*TSL* 3, 4). It is significant that, in this early set of anecdotes, sutra is twice cited as authority to confirm that nonsentient beings expound the Dharma—this by members of a tradition that was characterized as "a teaching outside the sutras." The *Avataṃsaka Sūtra* is reported as saying, "The earth expounds Dharma; living beings expound it; throughout the three times, everything expounds it." Yün-yen cites the *Amitābha Sūtra*, "Water birds, tree groves, all without exception recite the Buddha's name, recite the Dharma." All things were regarded not only as possessing Buddha Nature, a somewhat static quality, but also as being capable of teaching or manifesting the Dharma, an extremely dynamic quality.

Perhaps in part to accentuate the irony of nonsentient beings possessing Buddha Nature, Tung-shan uses objects and images of the most austere and inert sort as illustrations, nothing so endearing as water birds or even trees. An undefiled mind is perhaps what Tung-shan is referring to when he speaks of a place "without an inch of grass for 10,000 *li*" (*TSL* 58, 72). This image could only suggest a desert. Examples of similar images are "rice straw" (*TSL* 99), "grass that doesn't sprout" (*TSL* 103), and "a single reed stem after a fire" (*TSL* 92). Even the dead continue to teach. In *TSL* 32 Tung-shan tells his traveling companion that inside a roadside shrine (where someone would have been buried) "there is a person teaching about mind and nature." It has also been suggested that the inertness of the objects used as images emphasizes a nondiscriminating nature that is characteristic of the bodhisattva.[8]

Wandering, generally on pilgrimage, is another frequently encountered theme. This sometimes takes the form of visiting various masters and at other times is described as "entering the mountains." It would appear from the discourse records that pilgrimage during the T'ang was a major rite of passage for monks. These texts give us the sense that Ch'an monks were a very mobile segment of Chinese society. Through pilgrimage they seem to have been seeking to add breadth to their understanding and practice. Exposure to a variety of different masters would provide opportunities to observe various manifestations of the Buddha Mind. The importance of this practice in the case of Tung-shan is reflected in the preponderance of pilgrimage anecdotes that occur during his student phase. Well over twice as many exchanges occur between the student Tung-shan and the figures he meets on pilgimage than between Tung-shan and his master, Yün-yen. Many of the exchanges occur between Tung-shan and his almost constant companion, Shen-shan, a fellow disciple of Yün-yen. One (*TSL 25*) is with an old woman carrying water. These anecdotes give evidence that the belief that all beings manifest the Buddha Mind was taken seriously. An enlightened teacher need not be the only source or wisdom. The discourse records, rather than attempting to describe the truth of this claim, demonstrate it through the actions and words of the participants.

One practice associated with pilgrimage is that of "entering the mountains." On a practical level, the connection may seem quite obvious, since so many of the Ch'an masters had their temples on mountains. To visit them one could not avoid entering the mountains. However, journeys into the mountains seem to have been more than this. In the terse anecdotes of the discourse records, where the context is often left unstated, it is significant that mountain wandering, when it occurs, is mentioned explicitly. Furthermore, mountain wandering is often presented as a separate practice, an end in itself, with no mention of visiting teachers. For example, in *TSL 39*, when Hsüeh-feng tells Tung-shan that he is "returning to the peaks," their conversation concerns only how one goes there. There is no suggestion of visiting anyone. In fact, the manner in which mountain wandering is discussed in the anecdotes is suggestive of spiritual quest. The Chinese term often encountered in the discourse records, "entering the mountain" (*ju-shan*), is quite distinct from climbing or going to a mountain.

Of course, this term may not mean anything more than secluding oneself in a mountainous region, as Tung-shan's disciple Yün-chü did in *TSL 49*. But there are certain spiritual traditions in China, such as Mao-shan Taoism, where the aspirant is believed literally to go inside a mountain in order to undergo spiritual transformation. However one entered the mountains, the implications of the journey invariably seemed to be spiritual. Another word used when referring to mountain wandering is *yu* (e.g. *TSL 76*). This term is used in the *Chuang Tzu* chapter title translated "Free and Easy Wandering," where it implies a mental and physical freedom—clearly much more than travel for pleasure.

Mountains in China have been seen as a particularly powerful aspect of sacred geography. They are sometimes the dwelling places of the dead, or of local divinities. Yün-chü claims to be bothered by visits of "heavenly spirits" to his mountain hut (*TSL* 49). Mountains are filled with dangers, such as ferocious beasts, but they also hold a magnetic attraction to which the wealth of Chinese landscape painting and poetry bears testimony. In entering the mountains the pilgrim is often entering another reality. When Tung-shan encounters Lung-shan in his mountain abode, he is reminded that there are no roads into the mountain. Furthermore, Lung-shan seems to be as old as, if not older than, the mountain itself (*TSL* 23). In addition to being regarded as an external, physical sacred space, mountains have also been seen as images of internal, subjective sacred geography. In the *Lieh Tzu*, an early text associated with the *Lao Tzu* and the *Chuang Tzu*, we find accounts of journeys, rich in descriptions of natural scenery, that are explicitly identified as inner spiritual journeys. When we encounter such journeys in *The Record of Tung-shan*, that distinction seems to be left intentionally ambiguous, or the emphasis shifts freely from external to internal and back again. Is the Dragon Mountain on which Tung-shan encounters the monk Lung-shan his own Buddha Nature, to which no "paths" lead, or is it an actual mountain visited by Tung-shan in the course of pilgrimage? Possibly both.

In addition to being a characteristic of otherworldly mountain regions, sacred space also extends into the menial everyday world of monastic routine. A significant number of encounters in *The Record of Tung-shan* are set in various areas of the monastic environs that would not normally be considered appropriate for religious or sacred activity. Tung-shan confronts his disciples in such places as the garden, the rice paddies, the kitchen, the infirmary, and the tea fields. Either nothing and nowhere is sacred, or everything and everywhere is. That making soy paste (*TSL* 50), for example, can become an opportunity for manifesting Buddha Nature is simply another manifestation of Tung-shan's belief in the ability of all things to teach the Dharma.

As instructive as what appears in *The Record of Tung-shan* is what does not appear. Most conspicuous by his near absence is Ts'ao-shan, generally considered one of Tung-shan's principal disciples. He does not engage in dialogue with Tung-shan and is mentioned only as the recipient of Tung-shan's long *gāthā* entitled "The Jewel Mirror *Samādhi*" (*TSL* 116) and in the eulogistic summary of Tung-shan's life (*TSL* 120). Tung-shan's other disciples, such as Yün-chü, each appear in numerous encounters with their master. It is not clear why Ts'ao-shan should be so inconspicuous. Perhaps he was not, in fact, a close disciple, and his reputation is a result of his interpretation and development of the Five Ranks doctrine. Or perhaps his own lineage had died out so early that he was of less significance to the seventeenth-century compilers of the text.

Enlightenment, which historically has been one of the central concerns of Buddhism, is also rarely mentioned in *The Record of Tung-shan*. A "great awakening" *(ta-wu)* is noted only once (*TSL* 9), on the occasion of Tung-shan's own enlightenment when he saw his reflection in the river. Although Tung-shan is not shown to have induced a "great awakening" in anyone else, he does contribute to "awakening" in two cases (*TSL* 58, 64), and "insight" *(sheng)* experiences in two others (*TSL* 57, 81). Thus, if the exchanges in the discourse record were intended to induce enlightenment in those involved or were "enlightenment triggers," as they later come to be known, the compilers generally failed to note that fact. An alternate explanation would be that, contrary to later expectations, the anecdotes were not as concerned with enlightenment as with the path. In other words, it may have been thought more important to show the pure mind as it manifested itself in the world of phenomena than to note some discrete point or set of points in time at which peak experiences occurred.

Meditation, also central to the Buddhist tradition, is hardly mentioned, let alone discussed in any way that might be instructive. The question of the nature of *samādhi* or trance in meditation is raised by Tung-shan in *TSL* 61, and Tung-shan and a monk are described as passing away while sitting in meditation in *TSL* 80 and *TSL* 119.

Two other lacunae in *The Record of Tung-shan* should be noted in passing. Tung-shan did not engage in the type of disruptive activity for which Lin-chi was duly famous, such as blows and shouts. Where some Ch'an teachers befuddle their interlocutors with disruptive behavior, Tung-shan is gentler, using wit and mental dexterity that often leave his opponents speechless or faltering. There is also no trace of any awareness of the great Buddhist persecution of 845. Possibly most Ch'an Buddhist were less conspicuous targets for persecution than older, better-established Buddhist schools and were therefore less affected by the persecution. Or perhaps the persecution of 845 was of little or no significance to the editors of the discourse records, since they were so far removed in time from those cataclysmic events.

Terminology and Translation

Ch'an monks have at least two names of two characters each. Thus Ma-tsu is a sobriquet for the monk Tao-i; the latter is a clerical name. The sobriquet is generally the name of the location of the monk's temple. Tung-shan is literally "Cave Mountain," the site in northeastern Kiangsi where Liang-chieh's temple was located. The name "Ma-tsu" is one of the few exceptions to this pattern, since it is not a place name; it makes use of Tao-i's secular family name and means "the patriarch Ma." In Ch'an texts a monk is generally referred to by his sobriquet only, e.g., Tung-shan. When both names are used, I will treat the sobriquet as a place name, e.g., Liang-chieh (clerical name) of Tung-shan (place name). Otherwise, the place name will be treated as a sobriquet.

When monks addressed each other, they would generally not use either of the two names just discussed. Instead, they would use one of several titles. Since most translations of these titles make little sense, and where there is no comparable Western title, I have retained the transliterated Chinese or Sanskrit. The most common form of address between monks was *Acarya,* which appears in the Chinese text as *she-li.* This term was an abbreviation of *ah-she-li,* a Chinese transliteration of the Sanskrit term of address showing respect generally for a religious teacher. An almost equally common form of address between monks was *Ho-shang.* The origin of this term is unclear. An English equivalent might be "Oh Monk!" but since such vocative forms have disappeared from modern English, its use here would sound stilted. Thus the transliterated Chinese has been retained. A monk would often use the self-deprecating term "this old monk" when referring to himself. This form is by no means rigid, as the same monk often switches within a single passage to other forms of the first person (see *TSL* 3). Often, when talking about a monk in the third person, the Sanskrit term *śramaṇa (sha-men)* is used. This term originally referred to a certain type of ascetic wandering beggar in India who rejected the *Vedas* and sought instead to find satisfactory explanations of the universe and of life through reasoning and investigation. Eventually it became a general Buddhist term for one who has renounced the home life to practice the Buddhist way. *Shang-tso* (literally, "upper-seater") was originally used to designate senior monks but later became a term for matriculated monks in general.

Although we said earlier that Tung-shan had his center in Hung-chou, in modern Kiangsi, the title of our text identifies him as being from Jui-chou. This is because the name for that region, as for most regions of China, has changed several times. Shortly after the fall of the T'ang, Hung-chou was renamed Yün-chou, the regional name used in *The Transmission of the Lamp.* In the Southern Sung (1225) the name was again changed to Jui-chou, the name for the region used by the editors of our text.

The arrangement of the text as it appears in the *Taisho* Buddhist Canon has been slightly altered. The anecdote that should have appeared as *TSL* 12, according to the original order, has been moved to the end of the translation, becoming *TSL* 120. The reason for this is that the anecdote is quite different in content and style from the rest of the anecdotes and, judging by its eulogistic tone, may have been a memorial inscription. It is neither poetry nor dialogue, but a third person summary of Tung-shan's career. Thus it is more appropriate at the conclusion.

I am indebted to Carl Bielefeldt for first suggesting to me many years ago that a translation of *The Record of Tung-shan* was needed. The project took me to Japan, where, through the efforts and good graces of my sponsor, Professor Yuichi Kajiyama of Kyoto University, and his wife, I was able to spend three productive and delightful years. I am especially grateful to Professor Seizan Yanagida, who gave generously of his knowledge and time over the entire period of my stay there. I would also like to thank Professors Lewis Lancaster and Michael Strickmann for their support and criticism through the final phases of writing, and Gary Snyder, Mel Weitsman, and Roshis Hakuyu Maezumi and Robert Aitken for their consultation on questions of content and style. Special thanks are due to Peter Gregory for his support and advice and to Stephan Bodian for his careful editing of the text. A final word of gratitude goes to Taikan Shiomi Roshi who, through his generous contribution, has made possible the publication of this work.

Notes

1. For a discussion of Northern Ch'an and its influence on the Ox-head School and Southern Ch'an, see John McRae, "The Ox-head School of Chinese Ch'an Buddhism: From Early Ch'an to the Golden Age," in *Studies in Ch'an and Hua-yen*, edited by Robert M. Gimello and Peter N. Gregory, Honolulu: University of Hawaii Press, 1983.

2. Paul Demiévelle, *Choix d'etudes sinologiques*, pp. 118–19.

3. The term "concept" is used here and throughout this discussion in the sense of a general, abstract idea.

4. See Ruth Fuller Sasaki, *The Record of Lin-chi*, pp. 6–7.

5. This passage from the *Chuang Tzu* appears in chapter 23, "Knowledge Wandered North" *(Chih pei yu)*. See Burton Watson, *The Complete Works of Chuang Tzu*, p. 241.

6. For a detailed historical analysis of the use of the mirror image in early Ch'an see John McRae, *The Northern School and the Formation of Early Ch'an Buddhism*, Honolulu: University of Hawaii Press, 1986.

7. See note 45 of the translation.

8. There is a brief account of the evolution of this thought in Chinese Buddhist history in an article by William LaFleur, "Saigyo and the Buddhist Value of Nature, Part I," *History of Religions*, 13.2 (1973), pp. 93–128.

The Record of
Liang-chieh of Tung-shan
in Jui-chou

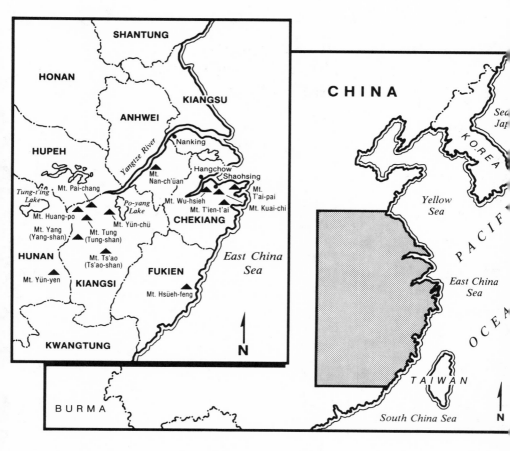

Ch'an Sites in Ninth Century Southeast China

1

The Master, whose personal name was Liang-chieh, was a member of the Yü family of Kuei-chi. Once, as a child, when reading the *Heart Sutra* with his tutor, he came to the line, "There is no eye, no ear, no nose, no tongue, no body, no mind." He immediately felt his face with his hand, then said to his tutor, "I have eyes, ears, a nose, a tongue, and so on; why does the sutra say they don't exist?"[1]

This took the tutor by surprise, and, recognizing Tung-shan's uniqueness, he said, "I am not capable of being your teacher."

From there the Master went to Wu-hsieh Mountain, where, after making obeisance to Ch'an Master Mo, he took the robe and shaved his head.[2] When he was twenty-one he went to Sung Mountain[3] and took the Complete Precepts.[4]

2

The Master set out on pilgrimage, and, going first to visit Nan-ch'üan,[5] he arrived when preparations were under way for Ma-tsu's[6] memorial banquet.[7]

Nan-ch'üan posed the following question for the assembly, saying, "Tomorrow, we will pay homage to Ma-tsu. Do you think he will return or not?"[8]

No one offered a reply, so the Master came forward and said, "He will come as soon as his companion is present."[9]

Nan-ch'üan said, "This fellow, though young, is suitable for being cut and polished."[10]

The Master replied, "Ho-shang, do not crush what is good into something mean."

3

Next the Master made a visit to Kuei-shan[11] and said to him, "I have recently heard that the National Teacher Chung of Nan-yang[12] maintains the doctrine that nonsentient beings expound the Dharma.[13] I have not yet comprehended the subtleties of this teaching.

Kuei-shan said, "Can you, Acarya, remember the details of what you heard?"

"Yes, I can," said the Master.

"Then why don't you try to repeat it for me?" said Kuei-shan.

The Master began, "A monk asked Hui-chung, 'What sort of thing is the mind of the ancient buddhas?'[14]

"The National Teacher replied, 'It's wall and tile rubble.'[15]

" 'Wall and tile rubble! Isn't that something nonsentient?' asked the monk.

" 'It is,' replied the National Teacher.

"The monk said, 'And yet it can expound the Dharma?'

" 'It is constantly expounding it, radiantly expounding it, expounding it without ceasing,' replied the National Teacher.

"The monk asked, 'Then why haven't I heard it?'

"The National Teacher said, 'You yourself haven't heard it, but this can't hinder those who are able to hear it.'

" 'What sort of person acquires such hearing?' asked the monk.

" 'All the sages have acquired such hearing,' replied the National Teacher.

"The monk asked, 'Can you hear it, Ho-shang?'

" 'No, I can't,' replied the National Teacher.

"The monk said, 'If you haven't heard it, how do you know that nonsentient beings expound the Dharma?'

"The National Teacher said, 'Fortunately, I haven't heard it. If I had, I would be the same as the sages, and you, therefore, would not hear the Dharma that I teach.'

" 'In that case, ordinary people would have no part in it,' said the monk.[16]

" 'I teach for ordinary people, not sages,' replied the National Teacher.

" 'What happens after ordinary people hear you?' asked the monk.

" 'Then they are no longer ordinary people,' said the National Teacher.

"The monk asked, 'According to which sutra does it say that nonsentient beings expound the Dharma?'

" 'Clearly, you shouldn't suggest that it's not part of the sutras. Haven't you seen it in the *Avataṃsaka Sūtra?* It says, "The earth expounds Dharma, living beings expound it, throughout the three times, everything expounds it." ' "[17] The Master thus completed his narration.

Kuei-shan said, "That teaching also exists here. However, one seldom encounters someone capable of understanding it."

Tung-shan said, "I still don't understand it clearly. Would the Master please comment."

Kuei-shan raised his fly wisk,[18] saying, "Do you understand?"

"No, I don't. Please, Ho-shang, explain," replied Tung-shan.

Kuei-shan said, "It can never be explained to you by means of the mouth of one born of mother and father."

Tung-shan asked, "Does the Master have any contemporaries in the Way who might clarify this problem for me?"

"From here, go to Yu-hsien of Li-ling where you will find some linked caves.[19] Living in those caves is a man of the Way, Yün-yen.[20] If you are able to 'push aside the grass and gaze into the wind,'[21] then you will find him worthy of your respect," said Kuei-shan.

"Just what sort of man is he?" asked Tung-shan.

Kuei-shan replied, "Once he said to this old monk,[22] 'What should I do if I wish to follow the Master?'

"This old monk replied, 'You must immediately cut off your defilements.'

"He said, 'Then will I come up to the Master's expectation?'

"This old monk replied, 'You will get absolutely no answer as long as I am here.'"

– 4 –

Tung-shan accordingly took leave of Kuei-shan and proceeded directly to Yün-yen's. Making reference to his previous encounter with Kuei-shan, he immediately asked what sort of person was able to hear the Dharma expounded by nonsentient beings.

Yün-yen said, "Nonsentient beings are able to hear it."

"Can you hear it, Ho-shang?" asked Tung-shan.

Yün-yen replied, "If I could hear it, then you would not be able to hear the Dharma that I teach."

"Why can't I hear it?" asked Tung-shan.

Yün-yen raised his fly wisk and said, "Can you hear it yet?"

Tung-shan replied, "No, I can't."

Yün-yen said, "You can't even hear it when I expound the Dharma; how do you expect to hear when a nonsentient being expounds the Dharma?"

Tung-shan asked, "In which sutra is it taught that nonsentient beings expound the Dharma?"

Yün-yen replied, "Haven't you seen it? In the *Amitābha Sūtra* it says, 'Water birds, tree groves, all without exception recite the Buddha's name, recite the Dharma.' "[23]

Reflecting on this, Tung-shan composed the following *gāthā:*

How amazing, how amazing!
Hard to comprehend that nonsentient beings expound the
  Dharma.
It simply cannot be heard with the ear,
But when sound is heard with the eye, then it is understood.

– 5 –

Tung-shan said to Yün-yen, "I have some habits[24] that are not yet eradicated."

Yün-yen said, "What have you been doing?"

Tung-shan replied, "I have not concerned myself with the Four Noble Truths."[25]

Yün-yen said, "Are you joyful yet?"[26]

Tung-shan said, "It would be untrue to say that I am not joyful. It is as though I have grasped a bright pearl in a pile of shit."

– 6 –

Tung-shan asked Yün-yen, "When I wish to meet you, what shall I do?"

"Make an inquiry with the chamberlain," replied Yün-yen.[27]

Tung-shan said, "I am inquiring right now."

"What does he say to you?" asked Yün-yen.

– 7 –

Once, when Yün-yen was making some straw sandals,[28] Tung-shan approached him and said, "I would like to have the Master's eyes."

Yün-yen said, "Where have yours gone?"

"Liang-chieh has never had them," replied Tung-shan.

Yün-yen said, "Supposing you did have them, where would you put them?"

Tung-shan said nothing. Yün-yen said, "Isn't it the eye that desires eyes?"

"It is not my eye," replied Tung-shan.

"Get out!" thundered Yün-yen.

– 8 –

When Tung-shan was taking his leave, Yün-yen asked, "Where are you going?"

Tung-shan replied, "Although I am leaving you, I still haven't decided where I'll stay."

Yün-yen asked, "You're not going to Hunan, are you?"

"No," replied Tung-shan.

"You're not returning to your native town, are you?" asked Yün-yen.

"No," replied Tung-shan.

"When will you return?" asked Yün-yen.

"I'll wait until you have a fixed residence," said Tung-shan.

Yün-yen said, "After your departure, it will be hard to meet again."

Tung-shan said, "It will be hard not to meet."

– 9 –

Just before leaving,[29] Tung-shan asked, "If, after many years, someone should ask if I am able to portray the Master's likeness, how should I respond?"[30]

After remaining quiet for a while, Yün-yen said, "Just this person."[31]

Tung-shan was lost in thought. Yün-yen said, "Chieh Acarya, having assumed the burden of this Great Matter,[32] you must be very cautious."

Tung-shan remained dubious about what Yün-yen had said. Later, as he was crossing a river, he saw his reflected image and experienced a great awakening to the meaning of the previous exchange. He composed the following *gāthā:*

Earnestly avoid seeking without,
Lest it recede far from you.
Today I am walking alone,

Yet everywhere I meet him.
He is now no other than myself,
But I am not now him.
It must be understood in this way
In order to merge with Suchness.

– 10 –

Later, during a memorial service before Yün-yen's portrait, a monk asked, "When the former master said, 'Just this person,' was it actually this?"

Tung-shan replied, "It was."

The monk said, "What did he mean?"

"At that time I nearly misunderstood the former master's intent," said Tung-shan.

The monk said, "I wonder if the former master actually knew reality."[33]

Tung-shan said, "If he didn't know reality, how could he have known such a way in which to answer? If he knew reality, why did he go to the trouble of answering that way?"

– 11 –

Because the Master was conducting a memorial feast for Yün-yen, a monk asked, "What teaching did you receive while you were at Yün-yen's place?"

The Master said, "Although I was there, I didn't receive any teaching."

"Since you didn't actually receive any teaching, why are you conducting this memorial?" asked the monk.

"Why should I turn my back on him?" replied the Master.

"If you began by meeting Nan-ch'üan,[34] why do you now conduct a memorial feast for Yün-yen?" asked the monk.

"It is not my former master's virtue or Buddha Dharma that I esteem, only that he did not make exhaustive explanations for me," replied the Master.

"Since you are conducting this memorial feast for the former master, do you agree with him or not?" asked the monk.

The Master said, "I agree with half and don't agree with half."

"Why don't you agree completely?" asked the monk.
The Master said, "If I agreed completely, then I would be ungrateful to my former master."

– 12 –

Yün-yen, addressing the assembly, said, "A son exists in a certain household who always answers whatever is asked."
The Master came forward and asked, "How big a library does he have in his room?"
Yün-yen said, "Not a single word."
The Master said, "Then how does he know so much?"
"Day or night, he never sleeps," replied Yün-yen.
"Is it all right to ask him a question?" asked the Master.
"He could answer, but he won't," said Yün-yen.

– 13 –

The prior[35] returned from a visit to Shih-shih.[36] Yün-yen asked him, "Since you entered the Stone Caverns, you shouldn't return just so, should you?"
The prior made no reply.
Tung-shan replied for him, "Someone had already occupied his place there."
Yün-yen said to Tung-shan, "And what will you do when you go?"
The Master said, "One should not break with customary etiquette."

– 14 –

Yün-yen asked a nun, "Is your father living?"
The nun replied, "Yes, he is."
Yün-yen asked, "How old is he?"
The nun said, "Eighty years old."
Yün-yen said, "You have a father who is not eighty. Do you know who that is?"
The nun answered, "Isn't he the one who has come just so?"[37]
Yün-yen said, "That person is still no more than the child or the grandchild."

The Master said, "Actually, even the person who has not come just so is no more than the child or the grandchild."

– 15 –

On the Master's first visit to Lu-tsu,[38] he payed homage and stood waiting. After a short time he went out and re-entered. Lu-tsu said, "Just so, just so. So that's how you are!"

The Master said, "There is definitely someone who disagrees."

Lu-tsu said, "Why do you concern yourself with eloquence?"

The Master accordingly did obeisance and attended Lu-tsu for several months.

– 16 –

A monk asked Lu-tsu, "What is wordless speaking?"[39]

Lu-tsu asked, "Where do you keep your mouth?"

The monk replied, "There is no mouth."[40]

Lu-tsu said, "With what will you eat?"

The monk didn't reply.

The Master said in his place, "He isn't hungry. What food would he eat?"

– 17 –

The Master visited Nan-yüan.[41] When he went up to the Dharma Hall, Nan-yüan said, "We have already met."

The Master then left the hall. But the next day he went up to the hall again and asked, "Yesterday I was the recipient of the monk's benevolence. However, I don't know where it was that we met before."

Nan-yüan said, "Between mind and mind there is no gap. They all flow into the sea of original nature."[42]

The Master said, "I was nearly overly credulous."

– 18 –

When the Master took his leave, Nan-yüan said, "Make a thorough study of the Buddha Dharma, and broadly benefit the world."

The Master said, "I have no question about studying the Buddha Dharma, but what is it to broadly benefit the world?"

Nan-yüan said, "Not to disregard a single being."

– 19 –

The Master went to Ching-chao to pay respects to the monk Hsing-p'ing.[43] Hsing-p'ing said, "You shouldn't honor an old dotard."

The Master said, "I honor one who is not an old dotard."

Hsing-p'ing said, "Those who are not old dotards don't accept honoring."

The Master said, "Neither do they obstruct it."

– 20 –

Then the Master asked, "What sort of thing is the mind of the ancient buddhas?"[44]

Hsing-p'ing said, "It is your very mind."

The Master said, "Although that's so, it's still a problem for me."

Hsing-p'ing said, "If that's the way it is, you should go ask a wooden man."[45]

The Master said, "I have a single sentence with which to express it, and I don't rely on the words of the sages."

Hsing-p'ing said, "Why don't you go ahead and say it?"

The Master said, "It's none of my affair."

– 21 –

When the Master was taking his leave, Hsing-p'ing said, "Where will you go?"

The Master said, "I will just roam about, without any fixed place to stop."

Hsing-p'ing said, "Will it be the Dharma-body or the Reward-body that roams about?"[46]

The Master said, "I would never explain it that way."

Hsing-p'ing clapped his hands.

– 22 –

The Master, together with Uncle Mi,[47] called on Pai-yen.[48] Pai-yen asked them, "Where did you come from?"

The Master replied, "We came from Hunan."

"What is the surname of the intendant there?" asked Pai-yen.[49]

"I didn't get his surname," the Master replied.

"What is his given name?" asked Pai-yen.

"I didn't get his given name either," replied the Master.

"Does he still administer affairs or not?" asked Pai-yen.

"He has ready assistants," said the Master.

"Does he still make his circuit tours?" asked Pai-yen.[50]

"No, he doesn't," replied the Master.

"Why doesn't he make his circuit tours?" inquired Pai-yen.

The Master turned, swinging his sleeves, and went out. The next morning Pai-yen entered the hall, and, summoning the two *shang-tsos,* said to them, "Yesterday this old monk was unable to reply to you with an apt turning phrase.[51] The whole night I could not rest easily, so today please provide me with a turning phrase. If it accords with this old monk's mind, then I will make provisions for congee, and we can pass the summer together."[52]

The Master said, "Please go ahead and ask, Ho-shang."

"Why doesn't he make his circuit tours?" asked Pai-yen.

"He's far too noble for that," said the Master.

Pai-yen made provisions for the congee, and together they passed the summer.

– 23 –

The Master together with Uncle Mi went to visit Lung-shan.[53]

The old monk asked, "There are no roads into these mountains, so what route did you follow to get here?"[54]

"Granted, there are no roads, so what, then, did you follow to get here, Ho-shang?" countered the Master.

The old monk said, "I didn't come following clouds or water."

"How long has the Ho-shang lived on this mountain?" asked the Master.

"I am not concerned with the passing of springs and autumns," replied the old monk.

"Which was situated here first, you, Ho-shang, or the mountain?" asked the Master.

"I don't know," said the old monk.

"Why don't you know?" asked the Master.

"I didn't come following gods or men," replied the old monk.

"What reason do you, Ho-shang, find for dwelling on this mountain?" asked the Master.

"I saw two clay oxen[55] struggling with each other, until they fell into the sea. Ever since then, fluctuations have ceased," the old monk replied.

The Master paid homage with a renewed sense of decorum.

– 24 –

When the Master was making a pilgrimage, he met an official who said, "I intend to write a commentary on the Third Patriarch's *Inscription on Believing in Mind*."[56]

"How will you explain the sentence, 'As soon as there is assertion and denial, the mind is lost in confusion '? "[57]

– 25 –

When the Master first set out on a pilgrimage, he met an old woman carrying water. The Master asked for some water to drink.

The old woman said, "I will not stop you from drinking, but I have a question I must ask first. Tell me, how dirty is the water?"[58]

"The water is not dirty at all," said the Master.

"Go away and don't contaminate my water buckets," replied the old woman.

– 26 –

When the Master was in Leh-t'an, he met Head Monk Ch'u,[59] who said, "How amazing, how amazing, the realm of the Buddha and the realm of the Path![60] How unimaginable!"

Accordingly, the Master said, "I don't inquire about the realm of the

Buddha or the realm of the Path; rather, what kind of person is he who talks thus about the realm of the Buddha and the realm of the Path?"

When, after a long time, Ch'u had not responded, the Master said, "Why don't you answer more quickly?"

Ch'u said, "Such aggressiveness will not do."

"You haven't even answered what you were asked, so how can you say that such aggressiveness will not do?" said the Master.

Ch'u did not respond. The Master said, "The Buddha and the Path are both nothing more than names. Why don't you quote some teaching?"

"What would a teaching say?" asked Ch'u.

"When you've gotten the meaning, forget the words,"[61] said the Master.

"By still depending on teachings, you sicken your mind," said Ch'u.

"But how great is the sickness of the one who talks about the realm of the Buddha and the realm of the Path?" said the Master.

Again Ch'u did not reply. The next day he suddenly passed away. At that time the Master came to be known as "one who questions head monks to death."

– 27 –

When the Master was crossing a river with Uncle Mi of Shen-shan, he asked, "How does one cross a river?"

"Don't get your feet wet," said Shen-shan.

At your venerable age, how can you say such a thing!" said the Master.

"How do you cross a river?" asked Shen-shan.

"Feet don't get wet," replied the Master.[62]

– 28 –

One day the Master was cultivating the tea plot with Shen-shan. The Master threw down his mattock and said, "I haven't the least bit of strength left."

"If you haven't any strength left, how is it that you can even say so?" asked Shen-shan.

"I always used to say that you were the one with lots of strength," said the Master.

– 29 –

Once, while the Master was on pilgrimage with Shen-shan, they saw a white rabbit suddenly cross in front of them. Shen-shan remarked, "How elegant!"

"In what way?" asked the Master.

"It is just like a white-robed commoner paying respects to a high minister."

"At your venerable age, how can you say such a thing!" said the Master.

"What about you?" asked Shen-shan.

"After generations of serving as a high official, to temporarily fall into reduced circumstances," replied the Master.

– 30 –

When Shen-shan had picked up a needle to mend clothes, the Master asked, "What are you doing?"

"Mending," answered Shen-shan.

"In what way do you mend?" asked the Master.

"One stitch is like the next," said Shen-shan.

"We've been traveling together for twenty years, and you can still say such a thing! How can there be such craftiness?" said the Master.

"How then does the venerable monk mend?" asked Shen-shan.

"Just as though the entire earth were spewing flame," replied the Master.

– 31 –

Shen-shan said to the Master, "There is nowhere that a friend[63] would be unwilling to go for the sake of friendship. Could you express the essential point of this in a few words?"

"Uncle, with such an idea how could you ever succeed!" replied the Master.

As a result of the Master saying this, Shen-shan was suddenly awakened, and from then on his manner of speaking became unusual. Later, when they were crossing a log bridging a stream, the Master preceded Shen-shan across, picked up the log, and said, "Come on over."

"Acarya!" called Shen-shan.
The Master threw down the log.

– 32 –

Once, when the Master was walking with Shen-shan, he pointed to a roadside shrine and said, "There is a person in there teaching about mind and nature."

"Who is it?" asked Shen-shan.

"If you can ask an appropriate question, Uncle, death will be completely cut off," said the Master.

"Who teaches about mind and nature?" said Shen-shan.

"While dead is living,"[64] added the Master.

– 33 –

The Master asked Hsüeh-feng,[65] "Where did you come from?"

"I came from T'ien-t'ai," replied Hsüeh-feng.

"Did you meet Chih-i?"[66] asked the Master.

"I will definitely partake of the iron cudgel,"[67] said Hsüeh-feng.

– 34 –

Hsüeh-feng went to pay his respects to the Master.

The Master said, "When you enter the door, you must say something.[68] It won't do to say that you have already entered."

"I have no mouth," said Hsüeh-feng.

"Although you may have no mouth, you should still give me back my eyes," said the Master.

Hsüeh-feng said nothing.

– 35 –

Once, when Hsüeh-feng was carrying a bundle of firewood, he arrived in front of the Master and threw the bundle down.

"How heavy is it?" asked the Master.

"There is no one on earth who could lift it," replied Hsüeh-feng.
"Then how did it get here?" asked the Master.
Hsüeh-feng said nothing.

– 36 –

The Master wrote the character for "Buddha" on a fan. Yün-yen saw it and, taking exception, wrote the character for "un-."[69] The Master altered it, writing the character for "not."[70] Hsüeh-feng saw the fan and immediately got rid of it.[71]

– 37 –

Hsüeh-feng was serving as the rice cook.[72] Once, while he was culling pebbles from the rice, the Master asked, "Do you cull out the pebbles and set the rice aside, or do you cull out the rice and set the pebbles aside?"
"I set aside the rice and pebbles at one and the same time," replied Hsüeh-feng.
"What will the monks eat?" asked the Master.
Hsüeh-feng immediately turned over the rice bucket.
The Master said, "Given your basic affinities, you will be most compatible with Te-shan."[73]

– 38 –

One day the Master asked Hsüeh-feng, "What are you doing?"
"Chopping out a log for a bucket," replied Hsüeh-feng.
"How many chops with your axe does it take to complete?" asked the Master.
"One chop will do it," answered Hsüeh-feng.
"That's still a matter of this side. What about a matter of the other side?" asked the Master.
"To accomplish it directly without laying a hand on it," replied Hsüeh-feng.
"That's still a matter of this side. What about a matter of the other side?" asked the Master.
Hsüeh-feng gave up.

– 39 –

When Hsüeh-feng took his leave, the Master said, "Where are you going?"

"I'm returning to the peaks," replied Hsüeh-feng.

"When you left, what road did you come out by?" asked the Master.

"I came out by way of Flying Monkey Peaks,"[74] said Hsüeh-feng.

"What road will you take now on your return?" asked the Master.

"I'll go by way of Flying Monkey Peaks," said Hsüeh-feng.

"There is a person who doesn't go by way of Flying Monkey Peaks. Would you recognize him?" asked the Master.

"I wouldn't recognize him," said Hsüeh-feng.

"Why wouldn't you recognize him?" asked the Master.

"He has no face," replied Hsüeh-feng.

"If you wouldn't recognize him, how do you know he has no face?" asked the Master.

Hsüeh-feng made no reply.

– 40 –

Tao-ying of Yün-chü[75] came to see the Master. The Master asked, "Where have you come from?"

"I came from Ts'ui-wei's place,"[76] replied Yün-chü.

"What words does Ts'ui-wei have for his disciples?" asked the Master.

Yün-chü replied, "When Ts'ui-wei was performing a memorial for the arhats,[77] I asked, 'Do the arhats actually come when a memorial is held for them?' Ts'ui-wei replied, 'What do you eat every day?'"

"Did he really say that?" asked the Master.

"He did," replied Yün-chü.

"It was not in vain that you called on such an able master," said the Master.

– 41 –

The Master asked Yün-chü, "What is your name?"

"Tao-ying," answered Yün-chü.

"Say what it was before that," said the Master.

"Before that I was not called Tao-ying," said Yün-chü.

"That's the same as this old monk's answer to Tao-wu,"[78] said the Master.

– 42 –

Yün-chü asked, "Why did the Patriarch come from the West?"[79]

"Acarya! Later, when you have a handful of thatch to cover your head,[80] should someone ask you that, how would you answer?" asked the Master.

"Tao-ying has erred," said Yün-chü.

– 43 –

One day, when the Master was talking with Yün-chü, he asked, "I have heard that the great monk Ssu was reborn in Wo as a king.[81] Is that so or not?"

"If it was Ssu, he will not become a Buddha," replied Yün-chü.

The Master concurred.

– 44 –

The Master asked Yün-chü, "Where have you been?"

"I've been walking the mountains," replied Yün-chü.

"Which mountain was suitable for residing on?" asked the Master.

"None was suitable for residing on," said Yün-chü.

"In that case, have you been on all the country's mountains?" said the Master.

"No, that isn't so," said Yün-chü.

"Then you must have found an entry-path," said the Master.

"No, there is no path," replied Yün-chü.

"If there is no path, I wonder how you have come to lay eyes on this old monk," said the Master.

"If there were a path, then a mountain would stand between us, Hoshang," said Yün-chü.

The Master said, "Henceforth, not by a thousand, not even by ten thousand people will Yün-chü be held fast."

– 45 –

Once, while the Master was crossing a river with Yün-chü, the Master asked, "How deep is this river?"

"Not wet," replied Yün-chü.

"Vulgar fellow!" said the Master.

"What would you say?" asked Yün-chü.

"Not dry," replied the Master.

– 46 –

One day, when Yün-chü was doing garden work, he accidentally chopped an earthworm. The Master said, "Watch out!"

"It didn't die," said Yün-chü.

"What about when the Second Patriarch went to Yeh-chou?"[82] said the Master.

– 47 –

The Master questioned Yün-chü, "An *icchantika*[83] is someone who commits the five heinous sins.[84] How can such a one be filial?"

"Only in so doing does he become filial," replied Yün-chü.

– 48 –

The Master described for Yün-chü the following exchange between Nan-ch'üan and a monk who was a specialist on the *Maitreya Sūtra*.[85] "Nan-ch'üan asked the monk, 'When will Maitreya descend to be reborn on the earth?'

"The monk replied, 'Maitreya is in his Heavenly Palace, and will descend later to be reborn.'

"Nan-ch'üan then said, 'There is no Maitreya, either in heaven above or on earth below.' "

Following up on this, Yün-chü asked, "If there is no Maitreya, either in heaven above or on earth below, I wonder who gave him his name?"

As soon as the Master was asked this question, his meditation seat began to shake. He said, "Acarya Ying, when I was with Yün-yen and asked the old man a certain question, the brazier shook.[86] As soon as you questioned me today, my body was covered with sweat."

– 49 –

After that Yün-chü constructed a hut on San-feng Mountain.[87] He passed ten days there without coming to the meal hall. The Master asked him, "Why haven't you come for meals these past several days?"

"Because regularly, every day, heavenly spirits[88] bring me food," replied Yün-chü.

The Master said, "Until now I have always said you were an exceptional person, but still you possess such views! Come to my place late tonight."

Later that evening, when Yün-chü went to Tung-shan's room, the Master called out, "Hut Master Ying!" When Yün-chü replied, the Master said, "Don't think of good. Don't think of evil. What is it?"[89]

Yün-chü returned to his hut and peacefully took up his meditation. From then on the heavenly spirits were completely unable to find him, and after three days, they ceased appearing.

– 50 –

The Master asked Yün-chü what he was doing.

"Making soy paste," Yün-chü replied.

"How much salt do you use?" asked the Master.

"I add a little from time to time," said Yün-chü.

"How is the taste?" asked the Master.

"Done," said Yün-chü.

– 51 –

Shu-shan[90] arrived just when the Master was giving his morning lecture. He came forward and asked, "Please instruct us using terms that have yet to exist."

"I won't reply. No one would accept it."

"Nonetheless, would it be of any value?" asked Shu-shan.

"Do you value it now?" asked the Master.

"I don't value it, and so there is no point in shunning it," answered Shu-shan.

– 52 –

One day during his lecture the Master said, "If you wish to know this Matter,[91] then you must be like the sear old tree that produces blossoms.[92] Then you will accord with it."

Shu-shan asked, "How would it be if one does not oppose it anywhere?"

"Acarya, that would be something on the side of gaining merit. Fortunately, there is the merit of no merit. Why don't you ask about that?"

"Isn't the merit of no merit that of a person on the other side?" replied Shu-shan.

"Someone could have a good laugh at such a question as you have just asked," said the Master.

"In that case, I would make myself remote," said Shu-shan.

"Remoteness is neither remoteness nor non-remoteness," said the Master.

"What is remoteness?" asked Shu-shan.

"It won't do to call it 'a person on the other side,' " said the Master.

"What is non-remoteness?" asked Shu-shan.

"That can't be determined," said the Master.

– 53 –

The Master asked Shu-shan, "What sort of person will be living during the Kalpa of Emptiness[93] when there are no human dwellings?"

"I wouldn't recognize him," replied Shu-shan.

"Would that person still have any ideas?" asked the Master.

"Why don't you ask him?" said Shu-shan.

"I am doing that now," said the Master.

"What is he thinking?" asked Shu-shan.

The Master didn't reply.

– 54 –

Shih-ch'ien of Ch'ing-lin[94] came to visit the Master. The Master asked, "Where have you just come from?"

"Wu-ling,"[95] replied Ch'ing-lin.

"How does the Dharma at Wu-ling compare with the Dharma here?" asked the Master.

"It's a barbaric land in which bamboo shoots come up in winter," replied Ch'ing-lin.

The Master said to an attendant, "Prepare some fragrant rice in a special crock and feed this man."

Ch'ing-lin swung his sleeves and departed.

The Master said, "Later this person will cause great consternation among men."

– 55 –

One day Ch'ing-lin came to take his leave. The Master asked, "Where will you go?"

Ch'ing-lin replied, "The adamantine disk[96] is not something concealed. Throughout the world it cuts the red dust."

"Take good care of yourself," said the Master.

Ch'ing-lin left with great care. The Master saw him to the gate and said, "Say something about leaving this way."

"Step by step, I tread the red dust. No part of my body leaves a shadow,"[97] said Ch'ing-lin.

The Master remained silent for a while.

Ch'ing-lin said, "Why haven't you said anything sooner, old Hoshang?"

"You've become very earnest!" said the Master.

"I have erred," said Ch'ing-lin, who then paid his respects and left.

– 56 –

Lung-ya[98] asked Te-shan,[99] "If I were holding the Mo-yeh sword[100] and intended to take the Master's head, what would you do?"

Te-shan stretched out his head toward the monk and shouted, "Huo!"[101]

"Your head has fallen," said Lung-ya.

"Ha, ha!" laughed Te-shan loudly.

Later Lung-ya went to Tung-shan's and told him about the previous incident.

The Master asked, "What did Te-shan say?"

"He didn't say anything," replied Lung-ya.

"Don't say he didn't say anything. Show this old monk Te-shan's fallen head," commanded the Master.

For the first time Lung-ya understood, and he admitted his error.

– 57 –

Lung-ya asked, "Why did the First Patriarch come from the West?"[102]

"I will only answer you when Tung Creek[103] flows backwards," replied the Master.

For the first time Lung-ya awoke to the significance of this issue.

– 58 –

Hsiu-ching of Hua-yen[104] said to the Master, "I am without a proper path.[105] I still can't escape the vicissitudes of feelings and discriminating consciousness."

"Do you still think there is such a path?" asked the Master.

"No, I don't think there is any such path," answered Hua-yen.

"Where did you get your feelings and discriminating consciousness?" asked the Master.

"I am asking you that in all seriousness," said Hua-yen.

"In that case, you should go to a place where there is not an inch of grass for ten thousand *li*," said the Master.

"Is it all right go to a place where there is not an inch of grass for ten thousand *li?*" asked Hua-yen.

"You should only go in such a way," replied the Master.

– 59 –

Once when Hua-yen was carrying wood, the Master stopped him and asked, "If we met on a narrow path, what would you do?"[106]

"Turn aside, turn aside," said Hua-yen.

"Mark my words," said the Master. "If you dwell in the South you will have one thousand followers, but if you dwell in the North, you will have only three hundred."[107]

– 60 –

Ch'in-shan[108] visited the Master. The Master asked, "Where have you come from?"

"From Ta-tz'u Mountain,"[109] replied Ch'in-shan.

"Were you able to see Huan-chung of Ta-tz'u?"

"Yes, I saw him," said Ch'in-shan.

"Did you see his outward appearance or what was behind that appearance?"[110] asked the Master.

"I saw neither his outward appearance nor what was behind it," replied Ch'in-shan.

The Master remained silent.

Ch'in-shan later said, "I left the Master too soon and did not completely acquire his mind."

– 61 –

After Ch'in-shan had been doing sitting mediation together with Yen-t'ou[111] and Hsüeh-feng, the Master brought them tea. However, Ch'in-shan had closed his eyes.

"Where did you go?" asked the Master.

"I entered *samādhi*,"[112] said Ch'in-shan.

"*Samādhi* has no entrance. Where did you enter from?" asked the Master.

– 62 –

T'ung of Pei-yüan[113] visited the Master. The Master went up to the Dharma Hall and said, "Cut down the host,[114] but don't fall into secondary views."[115]

T'ung emerged from the assembly and said, "You should know that there is one man unaccompanied by a companion."[116]

"That is nothing more than a secondary view," said the Master.

T'ung then flipped over his Ch'an cushion.

"Elder brother, what are you doing?" asked the Master.

"Only when my tongue has rotted out will I answer you, Ho-shang," replied T'ung.[117]

Later T'ung was taking his leave of the Master and was planning to enter the mountains. The Master said, "Be careful. Flying Monkey Peaks are steep and beautiful."[118]

T'ung thought about this and did not enter the mountains.

– 63 –

Tao-ch'uan[119] asked the Master, "What is the essence of shunning the world?"

"Acarya! There is smoke rising under your feet," said the Master.

Ch'uan immediately experienced awakening and did not go wandering elsewhere.

Yün-chü offered the comment, "Under no circumstances should you be ungrateful to the Ho-shang (Tung-shan), under whose feet smoke is also rising."

The Master said, "Treading the Darkling Path is persevering in practice."[120]

– 64 –

The Master was eating some nuts with Head Monk T'ai[121] during the festival of the winter solstice when he suddenly said, "There is something the upper part of which props up heaven, the lower part of which props up the earth, is as black as lacquer, and is always in motion. In the midst of this motion, it can't be grasped. Tell me where it is passing now."

"It is passing where its motion takes it," said T'ai.

The Master called his attendant and had him clear away the nut tray.

– 65 –

When the Master saw Yu *Shang-tso*[122] coming, he immediately rose and hid behind his Ch'an seat.

Yu said, "Why do you avoid me, Ho-shang?"

"I have always said that it was the Acarya who didn't see this old monk," said the Master.

– 66 –

While the Master was inspecting the rice paddies, he saw *Shang-tso* Lang[123] leading an ox.

"You should watch that ox carefully. Otherwise, I fear it will damage people's rice seedlings," said the Master.

"If it is a good ox, it shouldn't damage people's seedlings," said Lang.

– 67 –

A monk asked Chu-yü,[124] "What is the practice of a *śramaṇa?*"[125]

"His practice should be such that nothing is absent, but if he is conscious of his practice, it is wrong."[126]

Another monk reported this to the Master, who said, "Why didn't he say, 'I wonder what practice that is?' "

The monk subsequently carried this comment to Chu-yü, who said, "Buddha-practice, Buddha-practice."

The monk reported this to the Master, who said, "Yu-chou is all right, but Hsin-lo is insufferable."[127]

– 68 –

Again a monk asked, "How should a *śramaṇa* practice?"

The Master replied, "A three-foot head, a two-inch neck."[128]

The Master called his attendant and told him to convey these words to Ho-shang Jan of San-sheng Temple.[129]

San-sheng snatched at something in the attendant's hand. The attendant then returned and reported this incident to the Master. The Master approved.

– 69 –

Ho-shang Mi of Ching-chao[130] sent a monk to ask Yang-shan[131] the following question: "Right in this very moment, are you dependent on enlightenment?"

Yang-shan said, "There is no absence of enlightenment. Why fall into what is secondary?"[132]

Mi then sent the monk to the Master with the question, "What is the ultimate?"

"You must ask Yang-shan," replied the Master.

– 70 –

Ch'en *Shang-shu*[133] asked, "Among the fifty-two bodhisattvas, why isn't the stage of subtle consciousness seen?"[134]

"The *shang-shu* intimately sees the stage of subtle consciousness," said the Master.

– 71 –

An official asked, "Is there a practice for people to follow?"

The Master said, "When you become a man, there is such a practice."

– 72 –

The Master, addressing the assembly, said, "Brothers, it is the beginning of autumn, and the end of summer.[135] You may go east or west, but you should go only to a place where there is not a single inch of grass for ten thousand *li*."[136] After pausing for a while he asked, "How does one go to a place where there is not a single inch of grass for ten thousand *li*?"

Later this was related to Shih-shuang,[137] who said, "Why didn't someone say, 'As soon as one goes out the door, there is grass'?"

The Master, hearing of this response, said, "Within the country of the Great T'ang such a man is rare."

– 73 –

A monk said, "I would like to see the Ho-shang's original teacher. How can I do that?"

"If you are of comparable age, there will be no problem" the Master replied.

When the monk was about to reply, the Master said, "Don't tread a previous path. You should formulate a question independently."

The monk did not respond.

– 74 –

A monk asked, "How does one escape hot and cold?"

"Why not go where it is neither hot nor cold?" said the Master.

"What sort of place is neither hot nor cold?" asked the monk.

"When it's cold, you freeze to death; when it's hot, you swelter to death."

– 75 –

The Master went up to the hall and asked, "Is there anyone who does not reciprocate for the four forms of benevolence or respond to the three classes of beings?"[138]

The assembly made no response.

The Master spoke again, saying, "If one does not personally experience the meaning of this, how can he transcend the tribulation of birth and death?[139] If constantly and without a break you don't let any thought come into contact with things or any step come to rest, then you will accord with reality. You should strive earnestly and not pass the day at ease."

– 76 –

The Master asked a monk, "Where have you come from?"

"From wandering in the mountains," the monk said.

"Did you go to the top of any mountain?" asked the Master.

"Yes, I did," the monk replied.

"Was there anyone on the top?" asked the Master.

"No, there wasn't,"[140] said the monk.

"In that case, you didn't reach the top," said the Master.

"If it were the case that I hadn't gone to the top, how could I know there was no one there?" responded the monk.

"Why didn't you stay awhile?" asked the Master.

"I wasn't opposed to staying, but there is one in India who wouldn't permit it."

"I've been suspicious of this fellow from the first," the Master said.

– 77 –

A monk asked, "Why did the First Patriarch come from the West?"
The Master replied, "It is much like the chicken-scaring rhino."[141]

– 78 –

A monk asked, "If a snake were swallowing a frog, what would be the consequences of rescuing it or of not rescuing it?"

"If you were to rescue it," said the Master, "then you would not be seeing with your two eyes. And if you were not to rescue it, shapes and shadows would no longer be manifest."

– 79 –

A sick monk wanted to see the Master. Accordingly, the Master visited him. The monk said, "Ho-shang, why don't you rescue the sons and daughters of householders?"

The Master asked, "What sort of household are you from?"

"I am from an *icchantika* household,"[142] said the monk.

The Master remained quiet. The monk continued, "What does one do when the four mountains[143] close in upon one?"

The Master said, "Formerly, this old monk also passed time under a householder's roof.

"Will we meet again or not?" asked the monk.

"We will not meet again," said the Master.

"Tell me where I am going," said the monk.

"To a cleared field,"[144] said the master.

"The monk gave a sigh and said, "Take care of yourself." Then, while still sitting, he died.

The Master tapped him on the head three times with his staff and said, "You know only how to go, not how to come."

– 80 –

During an evening lecture, when the lanterns were not lit, a monk came forward to raise a question and then withdrew. The Master had his attendant light the lanterns and then directed him to summon the monk who had raised the question. When the monk arrived, the Master said to his attendant, "Obtain three pinches[145] of powdered incense and give it to this *shang-tso*."

The monk swung his sleeves and left. From this he gained understanding, immediately got rid of his excess clothing and possessions, and set up a food kitchen.

After three years he took leave of the Master.

"Be careful," said the Master.

At that time Hsüeh-feng, who was standing by the Master, asked, "With regard to this monk who has just taken his leave, how long will it be before he returns?"

The Master said, "He knows only how to go, not how to come."

The monk returned to the Monk's Hall and, taking his place underneath the shelf for his bowls and robes, died while sitting. Hsüeh-feng came to report this to the Master.

The Master said, "Even though he died like that, compared to this old monk, he differs by three rebirths."

– 81 –

The Master asked a monk, "Where have you come from?"

"From the stupa of the Third Patriarch,"[146] he answered.

Since you have come from the Patriarch's place, why is it that you still want to meet this old monk?" asked the Master.

"Because I am different from the Patriarch, but not from you, Ho-shang," said the monk.

"I want to be your original teacher. Is that possible?" asked the Master.

"Only if you first show your own face, Ho-shang," said the monk.

"I wasn't here just now," said the Master.

– 82 –

A monk asked, "What does it mean to say,: 'Having come upon it, he doesn't seize it. His mind aroused, he realizes its presence.'?"[147]

The Master joined his palms and raised them to his head.

– 83 –

The Master asked Te-shan's attendant, "Where have you come from?"
"From Te-shan's," replied the monk.
"Why have you come?" asked the Master.
"I've come out of filial feeling for you, Ho-shang," said the attendant.
"What is the most filial behavior in this world?" asked the Master.
The attendant did not reply.

– 84 –

The Master went up to the hall and said, "There is a person who, in the midst of a thousand or even ten thousand people, neither turns his back on nor faces a single person. Now you tell me, what face does this person have?"
Yün-chü came forward and said, "I am going to the Monk's Hall."

– 85 –

One time the Master said, "If you would experience that which transcends even the Buddha, you must first be capable of a bit of conversation."
A monk asked, "What kind of conversation is that?"
"When I am conversing, you don't hear it, Acarya," said the Master.
"Do you hear it or not, Ho-shang?" asked the monk.
"When I am not conversing, I hear it," replied the Master.

– 86 –

A monk asked, "What is proper questioning and answering?"
"When it doesn't come from the mouth," replied the Master.
"If someone were to question you, would you answer or not?" asked the monk.
"I've never been questioned," replied the Master.

– 87 –

A monk asked, "What does it mean to say, 'That which enters through the door is nothing precious'?"[148]

"It would be better to disregard that."

– 88 –

A monk said, "Since the Ho-shang has entered the world to teach, how many people have acknowledged him?"

"Not a single person has acknowledged me," replied the Master.

"Why hasn't anyone acknowledged you?" asked the monk.

"Because the realm of each individual's mind is like that of a king."

– 89 –

The Master asked a monk who lectured on the *Vimalakīrti Nirdeśa Sūtra*, "What is being referred to when the sutra says, 'He cannot be known by intellect or perceived by consciousness'?"[149]

"Those words praise the Dharma-body," replied the monk.

"That which is called the Dharma-body has already been praised," said the Master.

– 90 –

A monk asked, "Why can't one obtain the robe and bowl when one 'endeavors constantly to wipe it clean'?[150] What sort of person should obtain them?"

The Master replied, "One who does not enter through the door."[151]

"If one does not enter through the door, can he obtain them or not?" asked the monk.

"Although it's just as I have said, it isn't the case that he does not have them," replied the Master.

The Master also said, "Even to say 'From the very beginning not a single thing exists'[152] is similarly not a case of being worthy of obtaining the robe and bowl. Now speak! Who is worthy of obtaining the robe and bowl? You should present a turning phrase right here. What turning phrase will you present?"

At that time there was a monk who presented ninety-six turning phrases, but none was suitable. Finally he presented a phrase that satisfied the Master.

"Why didn't you say that earlier?" said the Master.

Another monk had eaves-dropped on these exchanges but had missed hearing the final turning phrase. Therefore, he sought help from the first monk, but that monk would not agree to talk about his answer. For three years he pestered the first monk, but in the end it still had not been explained to him.

One day, when he was ill, the second monk said, "For three years I have sought to be told that previous phrase, but I have not yet benefited from your kindness. Since I have not gotten it by peaceful means, I will use violence." With that, the monk seized a knife and said, "If you don't explain it for me, I will kill you, *Shang-tso*."

"Wait a moment, Acarya. I will tell you," said the first monk in terror. "Even if I were to bring them out, there would be no place to put them."

The second monk made his apologies.

– 91 –

A hut-dwelling monk,[153] who was not well would say to all the monks he saw, "Save me, save me."

Many monks spoke to him, but none of their solutions satisfied him. When the Master went to call on him, the hut-dweller called out, "Save me."

The Master asked, "What sort of salvation do you want?"

The hut-dweller asked, "Aren't you the Dharma-descendant of Yüeh-shan[154] and Yün-yen?"

"I humbly acknowledge that I am," replied the Master.

The hut dweller joined his hands in a gesture of respect and said, "I'm leaving you all," and then passed away.

– 92 –

A monk asked, "When a dying monk passes away, where does he go?"

"After the fire, a single reed stem," said the Master.

– 93 –

One day, when the monks had all gone out for general labor, the Master made the rounds of the monks quarters. Seeing a monk who had not gone out for general labor, he asked, "Why haven't you gone out?"

"Because I am not well," replied the monk.

"Have you ever gone out when you were in normal health?" asked the Master.

– 94 –

A monk said, "The Master normally tells us to follow the bird path. I wonder what the bird path is?"[155]

"One does not encounter a single person," replied the Master.

"How does one follow such a path?" asked the monk.

"One should go without hemp sandals[156] on one's feet," replied the Master.

"If one follows the bird path, isn't that seeing one's original face?"[157] said the monk.

"Why do you turn things upside down so?" asked the Master.

"But where have I turned things upside down?" asked the monk.

"If you haven't turned things upside down, then why do you regard the slave as master?" said the Master.

"What is one's original face?" asked the monk.

"Not to follow the bird path," responded the Master.[158]

– 95 –

The Master addressed the assembly, saying, "To know the existence of the person who transcends the Buddha, you must first be capable of a bit of conversation."

A monk asked, "What sort of person is he who transcends the Buddha?"

"Not a Buddha," replied the Master.

– 96 –

The Master asked a monk, "Where did you come from?"
The monk replied, "From making sandals."
"Did you know how to make sandals by yourself, or did you rely on someone else?" asked the Master.
"I relied on someone else," replied the monk.
"Did that person actually teach you or not?" asked the Master.
"If one accepts his teaching, there can be no mistake."

– 97 –

A monk asked, "What does it mean to say, 'Amidst the darkling, darken again'?"[159]
"It's like a dead person's tongue," replied the Master.

– 98 –

One time when the Master was washing his bowls, he saw two birds contending over a frog. A monk who also saw this asked, "Why does it come to that?"
The Master replied, "It's only for your benefit, Acarya."

– 99 –

"What sort of thing is the teacher of Vairocana[160] and the essence of the Dharma-body?" asked a monk.
"Rice straw and millet stalks," replied the Master.

– 100 –

A monk asked, "Of the three Buddha-bodies, which one did not fall among the multitudinous things?"[161]
The Master replied, "I was once very concerned about that."[162]

– 101 –

Among the assembly there was an old monk who returned from a visit to Yün-yen's. The Master asked him, "What did you go to Yün-yen's to do?"

"I couldn't do anything," replied the monk.

The Master substituted this reply: "Cliffs mounting layer upon layer."

– 102 –

A monk asked, "What is the meaning of 'blue-green mountains, the father of white clouds'?"[163]

"A place not densely wooded," replied the Master.

"What is the meaning of 'white clouds, the child of blue-green mountains'?" asked the monk.

"No distinction between East and West," replied the Master.

"What is the meaning of 'the white clouds hang about all day'?" asked the monk.

"Can't leave," replied the Master.

"What is the meaning of 'the blue-green mountains completely unknown'?" asked the monk.

"Nothing to watch," said the Master.

– 103 –

A monk asked, "What kind of grass is on the other shore?"

"Grass that doesn't sprout," answered the Master.

– 104 –

The Master asked a monk, "What is the most tormenting thing in this world?"

"Hell is the most tormenting thing," answered the monk.

"Not so. When that which is draped in these robe threads is unaware of the Great Matter, that I call the most tormenting thing," said the Master.

– 105 –

The Master asked a monk, "What is your name?"

"I," answered the monk.

"What, then, is the Acarya's host?" asked the Master.

"Just who you see answering," replied the monk.

The Master said, "How sad, how sad. The likes of people today are all just like this monk. They can only see themselves as the horse behind the donkey. That is to make the Buddha Dharma common. They still don't even understand the guest's view of the host. How could they perceive the host from the point of view of the host?"

"What is the host's view of the host?" asked the monk.

"That is for you to say," said the Master.

"What I can speak about is the guest's view of the host. What is the host's view of the host?" said the monk.

"To speak that way is easy, but to carry on that way is very difficult," the Master said. He then recited the following *gāthā:*

> Really! Look at the followers of the Way these days.
> Innumerable are those who acknowledge the main entrance.
> It's just like setting out for the capital to pay homage to the
>   emperor
> But only reaching T'ung Pass[164] and stopping.

– 106 –

The Master went up to the hall, and said, "The Way has no thought of accommodating man; man has no thought of accommodating the Way. If you wish to know the meaning of this, one is an old man and the other is not."[165]

– 107 –

The following incident was brought up. When Wu-hsieh[166] went to Shih-t'ou's, he said, "If in a word you can say something appropriate, I will stay. If you can't, I will leave."

Shih-t'ou took his seat, and Wu-hsieh left. Shih-t'ou immediately called, "Acarya, Acarya!"

Wu-hsieh turned his head back.

Shih-t'ou said, "From birth to death there is only this. What's the use of turning your head this way and that?"

Wu-hsieh was suddenly awakened and broke his walking stick.

The Master said, "Because Wu-hsieh was not a master at that time, it was too difficult for him to fully appreciate what had taken place. So although things happened as they did, Wu-hsieh still had farther to go."

– 108 –

A monk was taking leave of Ta-tz'u. Ta-tz'u asked, "Where are you going?"

"To Kiangsi," answered the monk.

"May I trouble you with something?" asked Ta-tz'u.

"What is it?" asked the monk.

"Would you mind taking this old monk with you?" asked Ta-tz'u.

"There is already someone who surpasses you, Ho-shang, but I can't even take him," answered the monk.

Ta-tz'u went to rest.

Later the monk told the Master about this. The Master said, "Why did you answer like that, Acarya?"

"How would you have answered, Ho-shang?" asked the monk.

The Master said, "All right, I'll take you."

– 109 –

Later the Master asked this monk, "What other teachings does Ta-tz'u have?"

The monk said, "Once, when addressing the assembly, he said, 'To talk about ten feet is not as good as accomplishing a foot. To talk about a foot is not as good as accomplishing an inch.' "[167]

"I wouldn't have said it that way," said the Master.

"How would you have said it, Ho-shang?" asked the monk.

"People talk about what they cannot do and do what cannot be talked about," said the Master.

– 110 –

Once, when Yüeh-shan was walking in the mountains with Yün-yen, a knife in his belt made a noise. Yün-yen asked, "What made that noise?"

Yüeh-shan drew out the knife and made a powerful slashing motion just in front of his face.

The Master described this incident for the assembly and said, "Look at Yüeh-shan. He inclined his body to deal with this matter. If the people of today want to clarify the Supreme Matter, they must first experience this kind of mind."

– 111 –

During an evening assembly, Yüeh-shan did not have the lanterns lit. He said, "I have something to say to you, but until the bull gives birth to a calf, I will not do so."

A certain monk said, "The bull has already given birth to a calf. It's only that you haven't told us what you have in mind."

Yüeh-shan said, "Attendant! Bring a lantern."

By the time the lantern arrived the monk had withdrawn and was lost among the assembly of monks.

Yün-yen recounted this incident to the Master and asked, "What do you think about that?"

"Although the monk understood, he was simply not willing to pay homage," replied the Master.

– 112 –

The Master recounted the following discussion:

"Yüeh-shan asked a monk, 'Where did you come from?'

" 'From Hunan,' replied the monk.

" 'Is Tung-t'ing Lake[168] full of water or not?' asked Yüeh-shan.

" 'It's not full,' replied the monk.

" 'After such a long period of rain, why isn't it full?' asked Yüeh-shan. "The monk didn't answer."

Tao-wu said, "It's full."

Yün-yen said, "Replete and becalmed."

The Master said, "In what kalpa has it ever increased or decreased?"

— 113 —

Yüeh-shan said to a monk, "It's said you know how to cast horoscopes. Is that true?"

"I must admit it is," replied the monk.

"Try to cast my horoscope," said Yüeh-shan.

The monk did not reply.

Yün-yen recounted this to the Master and asked, "What about you?"

"Please tell me what month you were born in, Ho-shang," said the Master.

— 114 —

The Master composed the "*Gāthā* of the Five Ranks, the Lords and Vassals."[169]

Phenomena Within the Real:
At the beginning of the night's third watch,[170] before there is moonlight,
Don't be surprised to meet yet not recognize
What is surely a familiar[171] face from the past.

The Real Within Phenomena:
An old crone, having just awakened, comes upon an ancient mirror;
That which is clearly reflected in front of her face is none other than her own likeness.
Don't lose sight of your face again and go chasing your shadow.

Coming from Within the Real:
Amidst nothingness there is a road far from the dust.
If you are simply able to avoid the reigning monarch's personal name,
Then you will surpass the eloquence of previous dynasties.

Going Within Together:
Two crossed swords, neither permitting retreat:
Dexterously wielded, like a lotus amidst fire.[172]
Similarly, there is a natural determination to ascend the
    heavens.

Arriving Within Together:
Falling into neither existence nor nonexistence, who dares har-
    monize?
People fully desire to exit the constant flux;
But after bending and fitting, in the end still return to sit in the
    warmth of the coals.

– 115 –

The Master went up to the hall and said, "When looking upon, what is
it? When serving, what is it? When accomplishing, what is it? When
accomplishing mutually, what is it? When there is the accomplishment of
accomplishment, what is it?"
    A monk asked, "What is 'looking upon'?"
    "When eating, what is it?" replied the Master.
    "What is 'serving'?" asked the monk.
    "When ignoring, what is it?" replied the Master.
    "What is 'accomplishing'?" asked the monk.
    "When throwing down a mattock, what is it?" replied the Master.
    "What is 'accomplishing mutually'?" asked the monk.
    "Not attaining things," replied the Master.
    "What is the 'accomplishment of accomplishment'?" asked the monk.
    "Nothing shared," replied the Master.
    The Master offered the following *gāthā:*

    The sage kings from the beginning made Yao the norm;
    He governed the people by means of rites and kept his dragon-
        waist bent.
    When once he passed from one end of the market to the other,
    He found that everywhere culture flourished and the august
        dynasty was celebrated.

For whom do you wash your face and apply makeup?
The sound of the cuckoo's call urges one home;
Countless multitudes of flowers have fallen, yet the cuckoo's
    call is not stilled;
Going farther into the jumbled peaks, in deep places its call
    continues.

The blooming of a flower on a sear old tree, a spring outside of
    kalpas;
Riding backwards on a jade elephant, chasing the *ch'i lin*.[173]
Now hidden far beyond the innumerable peaks,
The moon is white, the breeze cool at the approach of sunrise.

Ordinary beings and Buddha have no truck with each other;
Mountains are naturally high, waters naturally deep.
What the myriad distinctions and numerous differences show is
    that
Where the chukar cries, many flowers are blooming.

Can't stand head sprouting horns anymore;[174]
When the mind rouses to seek the Buddha, it's time for com-
    punction.
In the unimpeded vista of the Kalpa of Emptiness,[175] when no
    one is perceived,
Why go south in search of the fifty-three?[176]

– 116 –

Because Ts'ao-shan[177] was taking his leave, the Master transmitted
this teaching to him. "When I was at Master Yün-yen's, he secretly
entrusted me with the Jewel Mirror *Samādhi*,[178] thoroughly conveying
its essence. Now I am giving it to you. It goes as follows:

The Dharma of Suchness, directly transmitted by buddhas and
    patriarchs,
Today is yours; preserve it carefully.
It is like a silver bowl heaped with snow and the bright moon
    concealing herons—

When classified they differ, but lumped together their where-
     abouts is known.
The Mind, not resting in words, accommodates what arises;
Tremble and it becomes a pitfall; missing, one falls into fretful
     hesitations.
Neither ignore nor confront what is like a great ball of flame.[179]
Giving it literary form, immediately defiles it.
Clearly illuminated just at the middle of the night, it does not
     appear in the morning light;
It is a standard for all beings, used to extricate them from all
     suffering.
Although it takes no action, it is not without words.
Like gazing into the jewel mirror, form and reflection view each
     other;
You are not him, but he is clearly you.
Just as in the common infant, the five characteristics are com-
     plete;
No going, no coming, no arising, no abiding,
Ba-ba wa-wa, speaking without speaking;[180]
In the end, things are not gotten at, because the words are still
     not correct.
In the six lines of the doubled *li* hexagram, Phenomena and the
     Real interact;
Piled up to become three, each transformed makes five.[181]
Like the taste of the [five-flavored] *chih* grass, like the [five-
     pronged] *vajra;*[182]
Secretly held within the Real, rhythm and song arise together.
Penetration to the source, penetration of the byways,
Grasping the connecting link, grasping the route.
Acting with circumspection is auspicious;[183] there is no contra-
     diction.
Innately pure, moreover subtle, no connection with delusion or
     enlightenment.
According to time and circumstance, it quietly illuminates.
Fine enough to penetrate where there is no space, large enough
     to transcend its boundaries.
Being off by the fraction of a hairsbreadth, the attunement of
     major and minor keys is lost.

Now there is sudden and gradual because principles and
  approaches have been set up;
With the distinction of principles and approaches, standards
  arise.
Even if one penetrates the principle and masters the approach,
  the true constant continues as a [defiled] outflow.
Externally calm, internally shaking, like a tethered charger or a
  hiding rat;
The former sages, having compassion for such people, made a
  gift of the Dharma.
In their topsy-turvy state, people take black for white.
But when their topsy-turvy thinking is destroyed, the acquies-
  cent mind is self-acknowledged.
If you wish to conform with ancient tracks, please consider the
  ancients:
The Buddha, on the verge of accomplishing the Way, spent ten
  kalpas beneath the tree of contemplation;[184]
Like the tiger which leaves some remains of its prey, and like the
  charger whose left hind leg has whitened.[185]
For the benefit of those with inferior ability, there is a jeweled
  footrest and brocade robes;[186]
For the benefit of those capable of wonder, a wildcat or white
  ox.[187]
Yi used his skill [as an archer],[188] and there was the bowman
  who pierced the target at one hundred paces.[189]
Two arrowpoints meeting head-on,[190]—how is such great skill
  attained?
The wooden man begins to sing, and the stone woman rises to
  dance;
It is not attained in thought or feeling, so why reflect upon it?
A vassal serves his lord, and a child obeys its father;
It is unfilial not to obey, improper not to serve.
Working unobserved, functioning secretly, appearing dull,
  seemingly stupid—
If one can simply persist in that, it is called the host's view of the
  host.

– 117 –

The Master said, "In this Dharma-ending age people possess much idle knowledge. If you want to distinguish true from false, there are three types of defilement to be aware of. The first is defiled views. This is said to be not departing from a particular fixed view about the potential for enlightenment and thus falling into a sea of poison. The second is defiled emotions. This is said to be entrapment in preferences and repulsions, thus having one's perspective become one-sided and rigid. The third is defiled language. This is said to be mastering trivia and losing sight of the essential. The potential for enlightenment is thoroughly obscured. You should understand clearly that a disciple whose understanding is muddled and is going round and round in circles has not done away with these three types of defilements."

There is also the "*Gāthā* of the Essentials" in three verses. The verse "Rhythm and Song Performed Together" goes:

> One metal pin holds a pair of locks;
> The paths for the pin found, its function mysteriously simultaneous.
> The Precious Seal corresponding to the subtleness of the wind,
> Like the visibility of overlapping brocade stitches.

The second verse, "The Path of the Darkling Lock," goes:

> Interacting, darkness amidst light,
> One comes to feel that successful endeavor is difficult.
> One's strength exhausted, progress and retreat are forgotten;
> The metal locks pull each other like the meshes of a net.

The third verse, "On Not Falling into Distinctions Between Sagely and Common," goes:

> Principle and phenomena have no relation to each other;
> Reflected light cuts through dark mystery.
> Ignoring the wind, with neither skill nor incompetence,
> The lightning bolt is impossible to escape.

– 118 –

The Master was unwell and directed a novice monk to deliver a message to Yün-chü, saying, "If he asks whether I am well, simply reply that the transmission of Yün-yen's way will be interrupted. When you deliver this message, you should stand back. Otherwise, I fear he will hit you."

The novice monk acknowledged that he understood and went to transmit the message. But well before he had finished speaking, he was given a blow by Yün-chü, after which he remained silent.

– 119 –

When the Master was about to enter perfect rest,[191] he addressed the assembly, saying "I've had a worthless name in this world. Who will get rid of it for me?"

When none of the assembly replied, a novice monk came forward and said, "Please say what the monk's Dharma name is."

The Master said, "My worthless name has been eradicated."

A monk asked, "Although the monk is unwell, is there actually one who is not sick?"

"There is," replied the Master.

"Will the one who is not sick treat the monk?"

The Master said, "I am entitled to see him."

"I wonder how the monk will see him?"

"When I see him, there will be no perception of sickness," replied the Master.

The Master continued by asking the monk, "After I have left this filth-oozing shell, where will we meet?"

The monk didn't reply.

The Master recited a *gāthā:*

> Disciples as numerous as grains of sand in the River Ganges,
>   not one has gained enlightenment;
> They err in seeking it as a path taught by others.
> To eliminate form and eradicate its traces,
> Make utmost effort, and strive diligently to walk in nothing-
>   ness.

Then the Master had his head shaved, bathed himself, and put on his robes. He struck the bell and announced his departure to the assembly. Sitting solemnly, he began to pass away. Immediately the large assembly began to wail and lament. This continued for some time without stopping. The Master suddenly opened his eyes and addressed the assembly, saying, "For those who have left home, a mind unattached to things is the true practice. People struggle to live and make much of death. But what's the use of lamenting?"

Then he ordered a temple official to make arrangements for a "delusion banquet." However, the assembly's feeling of bereavement did not go away, so preparations for the banquet were extended over seven days. The Master joined with the assembly in completing the preparations, saying, "You monks have made a great commotion over nothing. When you see me pass away this time, don't make a noisy fuss."

Accordingly, he retired to his room, sat correctly, and passed away in the third month of the tenth year of the Hsien-t'ung era (869). He was sixty-three and had spent forty-two years as a monk; his posthumous name was Ch'an Master Wu-pen.[192] His shrine was called the Stupa of Wisdom-awareness.

– 120 –

From the end of the Ta-chung era of the T'ang (847–859), the Master received and instructed students at Hsin-feng Mountain.[193] After that, his teaching flourished at Tung-shan in Kao-an of Yu-chang hsien.[194] He expediently set forth the doctrine of the "Five Ranks" and skillfully instructed people of each of the three root types.[195] He magnificently proclaimed the single sound,[196] extending it to encompass myriad beings. He freely brandished the jewel sword,[197] cutting through dense groves of various false views. He wondrously harmonized the various teachings and widely propagated the Way, cutting off fruitless probings into all manner of things. Moreover, he gained Ts'ao-shan as a disciple. With profound understanding of the ultimate goal, he wondrously intoned this excellent design, a way that integrates lord and vassal and in which exists the mutual interaction of the Real and phenomena. Because of this, Tung-shan's subtle influence spread beneath heaven. Consequently, masters from every quarter unite in revering him. His lineage is called the Ts'ao-tung Lineage.[198]

Notes

1. The *Heart Sutra* (*Prajñāpāramitā Hṛdaya Sūtra*, T.250–57), an abbreviated Perfection of Wisdom text, is a body of thought central to much of the Mahāyāna tradition. It teaches, in part, the ultimate emptiness of all things, including the dharmas of the earlier Buddhist teachings. Thus, whereas earlier a meditator might have analyzed a particular experience into its components, isolating factors such as the relevant sense faculties and their objects, the Perfection of Wisdom literature instructs the Mahāyāna practitioner to recognize that those components, taken together as the reality of an experience, are in fact empty, and thus to be transcended. However, Tung-shan—ingenuously, it appears—reacts against the bald assertion that he has no eyes, etc. In *CTL* (T.51, 321b) Tung-shan's question does not concern his sense faculties, but the "rootless *guṇa*." See Chang, p. 58. *Ch'en,* the Chinese for *guṇa,* also means dust and, by extention, defilement. See note 58. Except for a slight difference in wording, the *TTC* is the same as the present text.

2. Wu-hsieh Mountain is located in Chu-chi hsien, Chekiang. Ch'an Master Mo (747–818), a member of the second generation of Ma-tsu's line, made this his center, becoming known as Ling-mo of Wu-hsieh. *TTC* 15, *CTL* 7.

3. Sung Mountain, which is in northern Teng-feng hsien, Honan, is the central peak of China's "Five Peaks" and the location of the Shao-lin Temple with its ordination platform.

4. According to the Sarvāstivādin *Vinaya (Ssu fen lü)*, T22, 567–1015, there are 250 precepts for a monk and 348 for a nun, though the latter number is conventionally quoted as 500.

5. P'u-yüan of Nan-ch'üan (748–834) began his study of Buddhism at the age of ten and was formally ordained on Mt. Sung in Honan at the age of thirty. His studies included the teaching of the Fa Hsiang, Disciplinary *(Lü, Vinaya),* Hua-yen *(Avataṃsaka)* and San Lun *(Mādhyamika)* schools. In the end, he took Ma-tsu Tao-i as his teacher and is regarded as one of that master's foremost disciples. After receiving Ma-tsu's approval, he set out for Nan-ch'üan Mountain (in modern Anhwei), were he spent thirty years living alone in a thatched hut. When he finally began to teach, he attracted several hundred students. *TTC* 16, *CTL* 8 (translated in Chang, 1971, pp. 153–63).

6. Ma-tsu Tao-I (709–788) was in the third generation of Liu-tsu Hui-neng's

line. He was born in Szechwan and is traditionally said to have been the major influence on the Ch'an of the Hung-chou region of China. Ma-tsu is regarded as having most fully developed that strain of Hui-neng's thought that emphasized the discovery of self-nature in the midst of daily activity. Also, the blows and shouts generally associated with Lin-chi can be traced to Ma-tsu. *CTL* 6 (translated in Chang, 1971, pp. 148–52).

7. A memorial banquet is a ceremony that normally lasts two days and finishes with a vegetarian feast on the day of death of the person being honored. Ma-tsu died on the fourth day of the second lunar month. Tung-shan apparently arrived on the first day of this particular ceremony.

8. There is a precedent for the belief that Buddhist masters attend their own memorial banquets. For example, in the first fascicle of the *Fa-yün chih-lüeh* ("A Concise Record on the Fate of the Law"), translated by Jan Yün-hua (1966, p. 18), there is a description of a memorial banquet for Chih-i (see *TSL* 33, note 3) held in 605. Though the number of monks in attendance was supposed to be exacty 1,000, their number increased by one during the course of the meal. The additional monk was believed to be Chih-i.

9. "Companion" is a common image in Ch'an texts for the physical (as opposed to the nonphysical) body. The term also denotes an attendant or someone to be relied on. In this case, the body (*rūpa* in traditional Buddhist terms) would be the attendant of mind *(nāma)*. Another example of this usage can be found in the *Record of Lin-chi:* "Followers of the Way, don't acknowledge your illusory companion; sooner or later it will return to impermanence." T.57, 498c; Sasaki, 1975, p. 15.

10. To be "cut and polished" is to be developed or perfected through teaching or discipline. An example of this usage of the image appears in the Confucian *Analects* 1:15.

11. Ling-yu of Kuei-shan (771–853), in the third generation of Ma-tsu's line, was the patriarch of the Kuei-yang House, the earliest of the "Five Houses of Ch'an." He left home to become amonk at the age of fifteen and began by studying the sutras and monastic discipline *(Vinaya)*. He eventually found his way to Pai-chang's center, where he become the leading disciple. In his book, the *Kuei-shan Ching Tse,* he discusses what he perceives to be the general degeneration of Buddhism in his time and proposes the means for its revival. Kuei Mountain was located in T'an-chou, modern Ch'ang-sha in Hunan. *CTL* 9 (translated in Chang, 1971, pp. 200–208).

12. Chung of Nan-yang is Hui-chung (d.775), a disciple of Liu-tsu Hui-neng. According to his biography, until he was sixteen, he never spoke, nor did he leave the immediate vicinity of his house. However, when he saw a Ch'an monk passing his house one day, he began speaking and requested ordination. As a result, the monk directed him to Hui-neng. He is said to have lived forty years on Po-yai Mountain in Nan-yang, modern Honan, without leaving. However, by 761 his fame had spread, and he was summoned to the capital, where he received the title "National Teacher" *(kuo-shih)*. *TTC* 3, *CTL* 27.

13. The question of whether nonsentient beings possess Buddha Nature and

thus, by extension, are capable of expressing Dharma—a major controversy in early T'ang China—grew out of differing interpretations of the *Nirvāṇa Sūtra*, T.374, particularly the line, "All beings, without exception, possess Buddha Nature." Hui-chung was a prominent spokesman for the belief that nonsentient beings are included under "all beings." On one occasion he cited the *Avataṃsaka Sūtra*, "The Buddha's body completely fills the Dharma Realm and is manifest to all beings." (*TTC* 3, 63a) Often cited in opposition to this is the following passage from the *Nirvāṇa Sūtra:* "Such nonsentient things as walls, tile, and stones lack Buddha Nature. All else can be said to have Buddha Nature." (T.12, 581a) Hui-chung could not have been unaware of this passage when he used wall and tile rubble as examples of the mind of the ancient Buddhas.

14. "Ancient buddha" is a term commonly used in Ch'an literature to refer to distinguished former masters, e.g., Yüan-wu Fuo-kuo's description of the Sixth Patriarch: "The Reverend Ts'ao-hsi was truly an ancient buddha," T.48, 807b.

15. Chuang Tze, when asked in the *"Chih pei yu"* chapter whether the Tao was found among the lowly, replied that the Tao "exists in the crickets, . . . in the grasses, . . . in tiles and bricks, . . . and in shit and piss."

16. In the Chinese the object of "no part" is left unstated. Yanagida translates it, "In that case, people would be completely without hope" (1974, p. 294), and has suggested that "salvation" or "nirvana" might be the object. It is also possible that the Dharma taught by nonsentient beings is the object here—which, in the end, is simply another way of saying "salvation."

17. *Avataṃsaka Sūtra*, T.9, 611a. The "three times" are past, present, and future, i.e., always.

18. The fly wisk usually consisted of the tail hair of some animal attached to a handle. According to tradition, the Buddha had approved of its use by the monks as a means of brushing off bothersome insects without killing them. However, because there was a tendency to use rare and expensive materials to construct the wisk, the Buddha stipulated that only certain ordinary materials be used: felt, hemp, finely torn cloth, tattered items, or tree twigs. Paintings of Buddhist monks indicate that in China this stipulation was ignored. In Ch'an it was a symbol of authority, generally held, when teaching, as an indication that the teaching was the correct Dharma.

19. Yu-hsien of Li-ling is in the northwest part of Ch'ang-sha in modern Hunan.

20. T'an-sheng of Yün-yen (780–841), although in the third generation of the Shih-to'u line, began his career as a monk together with Kuei-shan under Pai-ch'ang in the Ma-tsu line. He remained with Pai-ch'ang for over twenty years before going to Yao-shan, a disciple of Shih-t'ou. Yün-yen Mountain is in T'an-chou, modern Ch'ang-sha, Hunan. *TTC* 6, *CTL* 14.

21. "To push aside the grass and gaze into the wind" is a play on a line from the Confucian *Analects* suggesting the ability to distinguish the superior man from ordinary people. "The superior man's deportment is like the wind; ordinary people's is like grass. When the wind blows over it, the grass bends." *Lun-yü* 12: 19.

22. "This old monk" is a self-deprecating term often used by monks to refer to themselves.

23. The sentence quoted from the *Amitābha Sūtra,* T.12, 378a, is part of Shakyamuni's description of the Pure Land of Ultimate Bliss, the Western Paradise. Thus, since Yün-yen could not have been unaware of this fact, it must be assumed that he has tacitly equated this world with the Pure Land.

24. In place of "habits," *TTC* 6, 101b has "karma."

25. A similar exchange occurred between the Sixth Patriarch, Hui-neng, and his disciple Hsing-szu (d.740):

> Hsing-szu asked, "What must be done to avoid falling into [the practice of] stages?"
>
> Hui-neng responded, "What have you been doing?"
>
> Hsing-szu said, "I have not concerned myself with the Four Noble Truths."
>
> "What stages have you fallen into?" asked Hui-neng.
>
> Hsing-szu said, "What stages exist if there is no concern with the Noble Truths?" (*CTL* 5)

Tung-shan, whose lineage is traced back to Hui-neng through Hsing-ssu, appears indirectly to acknowledge the place he will assume in that lineage through his choice of words in this case. The Four Noble Truths, part of the earliest strata of Buddhist teaching, assert that there is suffering, its cause, its cessation, and a path leading to its cessation. Implicit in such a teaching is a belief in the existence of defilements or habits to be eradicated and of a gradual process or stages by which that eradication is achieved.

26. The Chinese term for "joyful" translates the Sanskrit, *pramuditā,* the name of the first of ten levels *(bhūmi)* attained by a bodhisattva in his ripening to perfect enlightenment. Though he attains sainthood at this level, certain defilements remain.

27. "Chamberlain" was a title used during various dynasties, including the T'ang, for the court official who waited on the Emperor and served as an intermediary between him and the court nobility.

28. In *TTC* 5, p. 97b, this line reads, "While Yün-yen was reading the sutras."

29. Instead of "just before leaving," *TTC* 2, 99b–100a, reads "just before the Master's (i.e., Yün-yen's) death."

30. Traditionally, a disciple was allowed to draw his master's portrait only when the master acknowledged that the disciple had received the transmission of his Dharma.

31. "Just this person" is a variant of "just this man of Han." The latter form is used in the earlier *TTC* version of the same incident (*TTC* 4, 100a). According to medieval Chinese legal custom this is the phrase by which a criminal formally confessed his guilt in court. Comparison with other occurrences of the phrase in Ch'an works (see *TTC* 8, 153b, and *TTC* 10, 202a) suggests that it expresses a thoroughgoing assumption of responsibility for one's being.

32. "Having assumed the burden" was another expression used when a criminal acknowledged his crime and personally accepted responsibility for it.

33. "Knowing reality" was used in a similar sense by Nan-ch'üan (see note 5). "Patriarchs and Buddhas do not know reality; mountain cats and wild buffalo know reality." *TTC* 16, p.297a.

34. See *TSL* 2.

35. The prior is the administrative head of a Ch'an monastary.

36. Shih-shih, "Stone Caverns," is both the name of a monk and the name of a place. This group of caves, located in Yu-hsien, modern Hunan, has long been popular as a place for ascetic practices, and it was in these caves that Tung-shan first met his teacher, Yün-yen (*TSL* 3). Because it was common for Ch'an monks to be referred to by the name of the place they became associated with, there was probably more than one monk named Shih-shih. The Shih-shih in this anecdote was probably the Shih-shih Shan-Tao who is mentioned in the *Record of Lin-chi* (Sasaki, 1975, p.4). According to accounts of him in *TTC* 5 and *CTL* 14, he was a mid-ninth-century monk who, at the end of the great Buddhist purge of 845, did not reassume his robes, but took up residence in the Stone Caverns of Yu-hsien, living as an ascetic. As a form of practice, he operated a foot-driven millstone. See *Blue Cliff Record*, case 34.

37. A possible allusion to the Sixth Partiarch's question to Nan-yüeh (677–744) "What is it that has come just so?" *CTL* 5.

38. Pao-yün of Lu-tsu Mountain in Ch'ih-chou (Anhwei). Ma-tsu's disciple (no dates). *TTC* 14, *CTL* 7.

39. "Wordless speaking" bears resemblance to Lao-tzu's "wordless teaching." *Tao te ching* 2 and 40.

40. "There is no mouth" appears to be a reference to the Perfection of Wisdom doctrine of the emptiness of all things, an issue already raised in *TSL* 1, and one that will be raised again in *TSL* 34.

41. Nan-yüan is Tao-ming of Yuan-chou (Kiangsi), a disciple of Ma-tsu. *TTC* 14, *CTL* 6.

42. "Between mind and mind there is no gap" bears resemblance to Lin-chi's "mind and mind do not differ." (T.47, 499c) This has also been translated, "Your minds and Mind do not differ" (Sasaki, 1975, p. 20). However, the Chinese *hsin hsin* does not make it explicit that two varieties of mind are what is intended here. *Hsin*, in addition to meaning "heart," is used to translate numerous Sanskirt terms having to do with mental phenomena, e.g., *citta*, "thought," *caitta*, "mental conditions (of thought)," *manas*, "mind." Thus the sentence might also read, "Between thoughts there is no gap."

43. Ching-chao is the environs of the imperial capital, i.e., Ch'ang-an. Hsing-p'ing of Ching-chao is included among Ma-tsu's disciples in *CTL* 8. The account there and in *TTC* 20 is the same as the one presented here; there is no additional information on him.

44. See *TSL* 3, note 14.

45. A "wooden man" is a puppet, one of the analogies used in the Perfection of Wisdom sutras for a bodhisattva in possession of the Perfection of Wisdom. For

example, in Edward Conze's translation of the *Perfection of Wisdom Sutra in Eight Thousand Lines* the following passage occurs: "An expert mason, or mason's apprentice, might make of wood an automatic man or woman, a puppet which could be moved by pulling the strings. Whatever action it were made to perform, that action it would perform. And yet that wooden machine would have no discriminations. Because it is so constituted that it lacks all discrimination. Just so a Bodhisattva performs the work for the sake of which he develops the perfection of wisdom, but the perfection of wisdom remains without discrimination. Because that perfection of wisdom is so constituted that it lacks all discriminations." (*Aṣṭasāhasrikā Prajñāpāramitā Sūtra,* Mitra ed., p. 443; Conze, p. 258). This image appears again at the end of the "*Gāthā* of the Five Ranks." *TSL* 116.

46. The Dharma-body (Skt., *dharmakāya*) is the absolute body of Buddhahood, free of all distinguishing features. The Reward-body (Skt., *saṃbhogakāya*), is the glorified body of Buddhahood, visible only to bodhisattvas. These two bodies are part of the traditional three bodies of the Buddha (Skt., *trikāya*); the third body is the Apparition-body (Skt., *nirmāṇakāya*), the body that appears in the phenomenal world, visible to all.

47. Uncle Mi is Seng-mi of Shen-shan, Tung-shan's fellow disciple under Yün-yen, thus called "Uncle" by Tung-shan's disciples. Shen Mountain is in T'an-chou (Hunan). *TTC* 6, *CTL* 15.

48. There is no additional information on this monk. The same account appears in *CTL* 14 with the name Pai-yen Ming-che of Ngo-chou. The account is included among those of Yao-shan's (751–834) disciples.

49. An intendant is an official sent from the central government to oversee local administrations.

50. The Chinese term for "circuit tour" is, literally, "to go out and come in," a conventional term for inspection tours of the provinces by an official of the central government, i.e., going out to observe the provinces and re-entering the capital to attend the Emperor at his court.

51. A "turning phrase" is a verbal response that demonstrates a turning of attention toward the reality of things or central truths. Such phrases were believed to reveal a person's level of insight and were a major component in much of Ch'an literature.

52. Presumably what is being referred to is the summer retreat, lasting from the fifteenth day of the fourth lunar month until the fifteenth of the seventh month. Thus, if Tung-shan and Shen-shan are to pass the retreat with Pai-yen, additional rice will have to be laid in.

53. Lung-shan (Dragon Mountain), also known as Yin-shan (Hidden Mountain, see *TTC* 20), is included among Ma-tsu's disciples in *CTL* 8. The mountain is located in T'an-chou. In both the *CTL* and *TTC* accounts of this encounter Uncle Mi, (Shen-shan) is not mentioned as accompanying Tung-shan. In addition, Tung-shan is said to be lost. Thus it would appear that he stumbled on Lung-shan by accident.

54. *CTL* 8 reads, "Where were you headed . . ."

55. Clay oxen were traditional ritual objects used to mark the beginning of spring, which, according to the Chinese lunar calendar, coincides with the beginning of the new year.

56. The Third Patriarch of Ch'an was the sixth-century master Seng-ts'an. Biographical information is very sketchy, the earliest extant account appearing in the *Ch'uan fa-pao chi* (Pelliot 3559), an early eighth-century work. The *Inscription on Believing in Mind (Hsin hsin ming)* is attributed to Seng-ts'an and can be found in *CTL* 30 (Suzuki, pp. 76–82).

57. In a note included with this anecdote in the *WCYL,* Fa-yen (885–958) offers a proxy answer for the official: "In that case, I won't make a commentary."

58. The Chinese term for dirty is *ch'en,* which commonly means dust or dirt, with implications of worldly or vulgar. Both Paramārtha (499–569) and Hsüan-tsang (600–664), in their translations of the *Abhidharmakośa Śāstra,* use *ch'en* for, among other Sanskrit terms, *rajas,* "fine matter," one of the categories of *rūpa-dharma* ("material elements"). This Sanskrit term is rich in denotations important both for the *Kośa* and for the present case. It is used for dust or dirt and, by association, for impurity. Related to the idea of impurity are such further denotations as menstrual discharge, darkening quality, passion, and emotion. The *Kośa* describes it as matter constantly in motion, unquantifiable, and as something that adheres and contaminates. It is frequently compared to the *kleśas,* defilements or obstructions to enlightenment. *Ch'en* is also used by Parāmartha in *Kośa* 1, as a translation for *viṣaya* ("sphere"), namely, the sources of stimulation for the sense organs; e.g., the sphere of sounds acts as stimulation for the ear. The implication here is that such stimulation is impure and polluting. Thus, while on one level the old woman is simply asking about any dirt that might be contaminating her water, on another level the question might be directed at the problem of spiritual impurity and pollution. This echoes Hui-neng's dispute with Shen-hsiu in *The Platform Scripture,* ch. 1, concerning the necessity of wiping dust from a mirror (Yampolsky, pp. 130–32). The question here is made particularly poignant in light of the traditional Buddhist doctrine of the innate impurity of women, a state that prevents them, *inter alia,* from becoming buddhas.

59. Leh-t'an was in Nan-chang hsien of Hung-chou, modern Kiangsi. "Head monk" *(shou-tso),* literally translates as "chief seat." Ch'u's identity is unknown.

60. "Path" here is the Chinese Tao, which can be understood in one of two ways. It can be read as the pre-Buddhist notion of the Way, e.g., the source of everything (as it sometimes appears in the *Tao Te Ching*) or the way of something such as Heaven, Nature, or man (as it occurs in both the *Tao Te Ching* and the *Analects* of Confucius). Or it can be read as a translation of the technical term for the Buddhist Path (Skt., *mārga*). Given the latter reading, one can understand this passage as praising the path and its fruit, Buddhahood, or simply as variations on a single theme, Buddhism.

61. "When you've gotten the meaning, forget the words" is a quotation from the "External Things" *(Wai wu)* chapter of the *Chuang-tzu* (Watson, p.302).

62. Appended to this case in the *WCYL* is the following variant:

Another text says that when the Master was crossing a river with Shen-shan he said, "You mustn't make a wrong step." "You won't get across if you take a wrong step," said Shen-shan. "How does one not take a wrong step?" asked the Master. "By crossing the river together with you," replied Shen-shan."

63. The Chinese for "friend" here is literally "wisdom" *(chih-shih)* or, in this case, "knower," a common term of address in Ch'an literature. In Buddhist texts it is used to translate the Sanskrit *mitra*, "friend," with the possible connotation of *kalyāṇamitra*, "good friend," a Buddhist term for a spiritual guide or teacher.

64. In Chinese the structure of Shen-shan's preceding response, "Who teaches about mind and nature?" allows it to be read either as a question or as a simple noun phrase, "the who that teaches about mind and nature." Thus Tung-shan's rejoinder, "While dead is living"—though a complete sentence in Chinese, since the subject need not be explicitly stated—is also potentially the grammatical completion of the previous response by Shen-shan understood as a noun phrase.

65. I-ts'un of Hsüeh-feng (822–908) was from Fu-chou (Fukien). He first expressed a desire to become a monk at the age of nine but was prevented from doing so by his parents until he was twelve. Much of his early life was spent visiting various masters throughout China. The present set of encounters apparently occurred during one such pilgrimage, which he made in the company of Yen-t'ou (*TSL* 61) and Ch'in-shan (*TSL* 60, 61). He didn't meet his master, Te-shan (note 73), until the age of forty, and he is said not to have gained enlightenment until the age of forty-five. At fifty he established his own temple on "Snowy Peak" *(Hsüeh-feng)* and is said to have attracted several hundred disciples. He was in the fifth generation of the Shih-t'ou line. *TTC* 7, *CTL* 16.

66. Chih-i (538–598) is traditionally regarded as the fourth patriarch of T'ien-t'ai Buddhism and founder of Kuo-ch'ing Temple on Mt. T'ien-t'ai in central Che-kiang. It would have been physically impossible for Hsüeh-feng to have met him.

67. The "iron cudgle" is probably the one associated with Yama, ruler of the hells.

68. Cf. Lin-chi, "Students come from all quarters. As soon as the host and guest have met, the guest offers a phrase to determine the worthiness of the host as a teacher." T.48, 500a; Sasaki, p. 23.

69. The fan would thus read "unbuddha(like)." *Pu* is commonly a negative prefix for verbs and thus imparts a verbal quality to the nouns it precedes.

70. The fan would now read either "not Buddha" or, possibly, "not unbuddha-like." *Fei* is commonly a negative prefix for nouns.

71. Neither *TTC* nor *CTL* provides any record of Hsüeh-feng being together with Tung-shan at Yün-yen's. Most likely, either the persona have been confused or this is an anachronistic embellishment.

72. According to the monastic regulations attributed to Pai-chang in the *Ch'an-yüan ch'ing-kuei*, ch. 10, the Rice Cook is one of the ten kitchen positions under the Chief Cook. The preparation of vegetables is delegated to another cook, and so on.

73. Hsüan-chien of Te-shan (782?–865) was a member of the fourth generation in Shih-t'ou's line. His family name was Chou, and because of his frequent lectures on the *Diamond Sutra,* he became known as "Diamond Chou." As a Ch'an master, he is known for his use of the staff to strike students. Te Mountain is located in T'an-chou (Hunan). (*TTC 5, CTL* 15) The present anecdote also appears in the commentary to *The Blue Cliff Record,* case 5.

74. Flying Monkey Peaks are in the mountains between Kiangsi and Fukien. Hsüeh-feng was originally from Fukien.

75. It was through Tao-ying of Yün-chü (835?–902) that Tung-shan's tradition continued the longest, at least into the seventeenth century. Tao-ying is literally "one who makes his heart the Way." Yün-chü (Cloud Rest) Mountain was located in Hung-chou. *TTC* 8, *CTL* 17.

76. Wu-hsüeh of Ts'ui-wei Temple made his center on Chung-nan Mountain in the vicinity of Ch'ang-an (Shansi) and was a disciple of Tan-hsia T'ien-jan (738–824) in Shih-t'ou's line. *TTC 5, CTL* 14.

77. An arhat is the accomplished saint of the pre-Mahāyāna Buddhist traditions. An arhat has understood what is necessary for his own personal salvation and, having accomplished what was necessary, will enter final nirvana at death. The apparent issue here is the same as that raised in *TSL* 2 and 11, i.e., whether a deceased saint is cognizant of honors offered him by the living. The exchange between the monk and Ts'ui-wei recounted here also appears in the section on Ts'ui-wei in *CTL* 14. Directly preceding it is the following exchange:

> Because the Master (Ts'ui-wei) was performing a memorial for the arhats, a monk said, "Tan-hsia (Ts'ui-wei's master) burned a wooden Buddha, so why do you, Ho-shang, perform a memorial for the arhats?'
>
> The Master replied, 'Burned, yet not burned; honored, yet indifferent to being honored.'

78. Yüan-chih of Tao-wu Mountain (769–835) was the brother of Tung-shan's master, Yün-yen, and became Tung-shan's teacher following Yün-yen's death. Both brothers were disciples of Yao-shan. Tao-wu Mountain is in T'an-chou (*TTC* 5, *CTL* 14). In the versions of this anecdote contained in *TTC* 8 and *CTL* 17, Tung-shan does not claim to have given his answer to Tao-wu, but to Yün-yen.

79. The question "Why did the Patriarch come from the West?" is one of the most common in the discourse records. The patriarch who came from the West was the First Ch'an Patriarch in China, Bodhidharma (d.529). The traditional, though highly legendary, account of Bodhidharma's life is found in *The Biographies of Eminent Monks (Hsü kao-seng chuan,* T.2060), compiled around 655. There, Bodhidharma is described as being the third son in a south Indian Brahmin family. Around the beginning of the sixth century he is said to have traveled by sea to south China in order to transmit the Buddha's teaching.

80. "A handful of thatch" suggests a small village temple or hut, which Yün-chü might later occupy as master.

81. "The great monk Ssu" is Hui-ssu of Nan-yüeh (515–577), Chih-i's teacher and an advocate of the teachings of the *Lotus Sutra*. Tung-shan's question concerns a legend prevalent in both China and Japan, according to which Hui-ssu was reborn in Japan *(Wo)* as the great Buddhist ruler, Prince Shotoku (574–622).

82. The Second Patriarch was Bodhidharma's successor, Hui-k'o (487–593). See *TTC* 2, *CTL* 3. The issue raised here by Tung-shan is an incident referred to in *TTC* 2. Hui-k'o went to Yeh-chou where he was arrested and executed for interfering with a sermon by Dharma Master Pien-ho. This was interpreted as expiation of karma incurred in a previous life. Though the nature of Hui-k'o's karma-producing act is not mentioned, it apparently bears similarity to Yün-chü's injuring the earthworm. Yeh-chou was in eastern Wei.

83. According to the *Nirvāṇa Sūtra* (T.347), ch. 19, "An *icchantika* is one who does not believe in the existence of causes and conditions, is devoid of shame, does not believe in karmic reward, does not see that this world is connected to the future, is not drawn to good friends, and does not accord with the Buddha's teachings and rules." Also, in ch. 5, "An *icchantika* has cut off all his good roots."

84. The five heinous sins are to kill one's father, to kill one's mother, to kill an arhat, to disrupt the monastic community, and to draw the Buddha's blood. The first two are interpreted as being ungrateful for the nurturance and care given by one's parents; the following three are regarded as despising the field of merit.

85. The *Maitreya Sūtra* (T.454), translated by Kumārajīva (344–413), concerns the Buddha yet to come, Maitreya. He is said to be dwelling in the Heavenly Palace in Tuṣita Heaven, the fourth of the six heavens in the Realm of Desire. He will reside there for a total of 5,670,000,000 years before descending as a savior.

86. It is not clear what exchange Tung-shan is referring to here, but it appears to be one in which Tung-shan demonstrates his worthiness as Yün-yen's heir. The importance of that event is confirmed by the shaking of the brazier. Likewise, Tung-shan's transmission to Yün-chü is confirmed by the shaking of his meditation seat.

87. The location of San-feng (Three Peaks) Mountain is uncertain, but it would seem to be in the vicinity of Tung-shan's center, since Yün-chü was apparently close enough to return for his meals.

88. "Heavenly spirits" *(t'ien shen)* are distinguished in Chinese tradition from "ghosts of the earth" *(ti ch'i)*. In the cosmology inherited from India, the heavenly spirits are the gods ruled by Indra who dwells in the heavens of the Realm of Desire.

89. Variations of this admonition appear several times elsewhere in Ch'an literature. Perhaps the best known instance is in the Sung edition of the *Platform Sutra of the Sixth Patriarch,* T.2008, where Hui-neng addresses *Shang-tso* Tao-ming, "Don't think of good. Don't think of evil. Just in this moment, what is your original face?" See Wang Mou-lam, p.21. This incident is also recorded in case 23 of the *Gateless Gate (Wu men kuan)*. However, it is not recorded in the earlier Tun-huang edition (T'ang) of the *Platform Sutra,* T.2007. One of the earliest

extant examples of the admonition seems to be the one in Hui-neng's biography in *TTC* 2 (952 A.D.), where it is part of a sermon. "If you wish to know the mind essence, simply don't think about any good or evil, and therby gain entry to Mind." In *CTL* 8, Nan-ch'üan says: "Not thinking of good, not thinking of evil, when no thought arises, then my original face appears." The present anecdote is not recorded in the Tung-shan section of *CTL* 15.

90. K'uang-jen of Shu-shan (837–909) established his temple on Mt. Shu, which is located in Fu-chou. *TTC* 8, *CTL* 17.

91. The "Matter," also sometimes the "Great Matter," refers to the essential, ineffable truth of Buddhism. In the chapter on "Skillful Means" *(fang pien)* in the *Lotus Sutra,* the term appears as "the one Great Causal Matter": "This Law [which the buddhas expound] cannot be understood by powers of thought or discrimination. Only the buddhas can discern it. Why? Because the various buddhas, the world honored ones, only on account of the one Great Causal Matter, appear in the world. Śāriputra, why do I say, the various buddhas, the world honored ones, only on account of the one Great Causal Matter, appear in the world? The various buddhas, the world honored ones, appear in the world because they want to induce all living beings to open Buddha-wisdom and to cause them to attain purity." (T.262, 7a; Kato, p.59) Hui-neng quotes from this passage while explaining the *Lotus Sutra* as teaching the "one-vehicle Dharma". In discussing this passage he says, "To discard false views, this is the one Great Causal Matter." (T.48, 342c; Yampolsky, p.166) Lin-chi also refers to the "Great Matter" in the following passage: "If I were to demonstrate the Great Matter in strict keeping with the the teaching of the Patriarch School, I simply couldn't open my mouth, and there wouldn't be any place for you to find footing." T.47, 469b; Sasaki, p. 1.

92. "The sear old tree that produces blossoms" is a traditional Chinese literary image, e.g., "Smoke rising over cold ashes; flowers blooming on an already sear old tree" and "The brillance of his rhetoric is capable of making an emptied stream flow again, and a sear old tree put forth blossoms."

93. According to the *Abhidharmakośa Śāstra,* ch. 12, the Kalpa of Emptiness is one of four time periods that comprise one Great Kalpa *(mahākalpa),* the length of time a world-system exists from creation total destruction. Each of the four kalpas is subdivided into twenty "small kalpas" *(antara kalpa).* The four kalpas are cyclic, occurring in the following order: (1) the Kalpa of Evolution *(vivarta),* (2) the Kalpa of Existing *(vivarta-sthāyin),* (3) the Kalpa of Dissolution *(samvarta),* (4) the Kalpa of Emptiness *(samvarta-sthāyin).* After the Kalpa of Emptiness there is another Kalpa of Evolution, and so on. During the Kalpa of Emptiness there is the total extinction of everything below the Fourth *Dhyana* Heaven in the Form Realm.

94. Shih-ch'ien of Ch'ing-lin (d.904?), also known as "Tung-shan the Latter," was one of Tung-shan's eight principle disciples. After living in seclusion for many years, he recalled Tung-shan's parting words to him, "You should benefit the masses of untaught. Why fix on trivial matters?" and left his retreat. He then went to Sui-chou and was invited to dwell in a place called "Green Wood" *(ch'ing-*

lin). Hence he came to be known as the "Ho-shang of the Green Wood." *TTC* 8, *CTL* 17.

95. Wu-ling is a district west of Tung-t'ing Lake in Hunan Province, modern Ch'ang-te. Te-shan was active in this district at the time Ch'ing-lin might have been there. Thus, the following question may refer to the teaching of Te-shan.

96. The "adamantine disk"—one of the seven treasures bestowed by Śakra on a *cakravartin* (wheel-turning king) at his ascension to power—is a sunlike object, that rises in the East and emits light. It is said to aid such a king in ruling. See *Abhidharmakośa Śāstra,* Ch. 11, and the *Sutra of Miscellaneous Similies* (*Tsa pi-yu ching,* T.4, 530c).

97. Ch'ing-lin is using the adamantine disk, which leaves no shadow, as an image for himself.

98. Lung-ya is the name of a mountain in Hunan just south of Tung-t'ing Lake. Chü-tun of Lung-ya (835–923) is associated with Miao-chi Monastery, which was located on this mountain. He appears in the *Record of Lin-chi* (T.47, 505b; Sasaki, p.48) where he questions Lin-chi and visits Ts'ui-wei. Also see *TTC* 8, and *Blue Cliff Record,* case 20.

99. See note 73.

100. The "Mo-yeh sword" was a legendary weapon belonging to King Ho-lu of Wu (515–496 B.C.).

101. "Huo" is the sound of a boat being pulled through the water. Here, it is apparently intended to be the sound of the sword cutting Te-shan's neck.

102. Lung-ya asks the same question of both Ts'ui-wei and Lin-chi. (See the *Record of Lin-chi,* T.47, 505b; Sasaki, p. 48.) In these two encounters Lung-ya is given a blow with a stick. Tung-shan's response is more benign. Cf. *TSL* 42.

103. Tung Creek is presumably a creek in the vicinity of Tung Mountain, though the *Shui Ching* records the existence of a creek by this name in Hunan, so called for its origin in the Great Western Cave (*ta hsi tung).*

104. Hsiu-ching of Hua-yen Temple is included among Tung-shan's disciples. He made his center at the Hua-yen Temple in Ch'ang-an, the imperial capital, and is recorded as having had over three hundred disciples. The Emperor bestowed on him the name "Great Master Precious Wisdom." *TTC* 8, *CTL* 17.

105. The word *li,* translated here as "proper," carries with it much more than such a simple rendering can convey. Derived from a term that described the cutting of jade along its veins, it came to mean the ability to govern or regulate based on an understanding of the fundamental arrangement of things. Hence, in the philosophical texts such as the *Mencius,* it has the sense of natural principle or law. In the present case it could describe a way of living without obstructions in tune with natural principles.

106. "If we met on a narrow path . . ." is a standard predicament in Ch'an anecdotes, acting as a metaphor for an unavoidable and impossible situation, the path being so narrow as not to allow two people to pass safely. Retreat is apparently not considered a viable alternative.

107. Hua-yen eventually went north to Ch'ang-an, where he was said to have had three hundred followers. This prediction probably reflected the historical

fact of the greater wealth and higher standard of living of the South at this time and is, therefore, not a comment on Hua-yen's ability to attract followers.

108. Wen-sui of Ch'in-shan was born in Fu-chou (Fukien) and took his vows under Huan-chung of Ta-tz'u Mountain in Hang-chou. He accompanied Yen-t'ou (see *TSL* 61) and Hsüeh-feng (see *TSL* 33) on a pilgrimage. Although these two received Te-shan's seal, Wen-sui did not, and he continued on to Tung-shan's, where he received the latter's seal. At the age of twenty-seven he established his own center on Ch'in Mountain in Li-chou (Hunan). *TTC* 8, *CTL* 17.

109. Ta-tz'u is a mountain in Hang-chou (Chekiang) on which there is also a temple of that name. Huan-chung (780–861) was the master of this temple. Born in Ho-tung P'u-pan (P'u-chou, Shansi), he began as a student of the *Vinaya (The Book of Discipline)* but later met Pai-chang and recognized him as his master. This places him in the Ma-tsu line. Defrocked in 844 during the suppression of Buddhism, he reassumed his robes following the death of Emperor Wu Tsung in 847. (*TTC* 17, *CTL* 9) Although Ch'in-shan's response is interpreted to mean that he came from the mountain, it is equally possible to read the Chinese to mean that he came from the temple or from Huan-chung.

110. In the *Diamond Sutra* the Buddha says, "Those who see me by my form . . . are not able to see the Tathāgata." (T.8, 752a; Conze, 1958, p.63)

111. Ch'uan-hou of Yen-t'ou (828–887) was born in Ch'uan-chou (Hopei). He took his vows at Hsi-ming Temple, the main temple of the lineage concentrating on the Buddhist Discipline *(Four-part Vinaya; Ssu-fen lü)*. He later participated in a pilgrimage with Hsüeh-feng and Ch'in-shan, eventually meeting Te-shan and, along with Hsüeh-feng, inheriting his lineage. During the persecutions that began in 845, he is said to have worked as a ferryman. He was apparently slashed to death by bandits while seated in meditation. *TTC* 7, *CTL* 16.

112. *Samādhi* is etymologically related to the Greek "synthesis," here denoting a progressive concentration of mind. It was brought about by focusing on an external object, followed by a process of introversion that ultimately terminated in a complete cessation of sensory perception and consciousness. This was the traditional process of meditation described at various points throughout the *Abhidharmakośa*. *Samādhi* was generally criticized by Ch'an masters as a misguided Hinayāna practice.

113. T'ung Chueh-t'ou of Pei-yüan is included among Tung-shan's disciples in *CTL* 17.

114. "Host" and "guest" are popular shibboleths found throughout Ch'an texts. "Host" often occurs juxtaposed to "guest" and on one level suggests the Ch'an notion of one's original or essential nature. "Guest," in contrast, suggests the conventional, everyday self as seen, for example, from society's perspective. See *TSL* 105.

115. "Secondary views" are the relativistic views one generally adheres to in one's ordinary activities, as opposed to "the primary view," things seen in their original or absolute nature. See *Li-tai fa-pao chi* 25 and 28.

116. See *TSL* 2.

117. According to *CTL* 17, T'ung holds this exchange not with Tung-shan,

but with Shan-hui of Chia-shan (805–881). The incident is not recorded in the *TTC*.

118. T'ung is presumably on his way to Fu-chou, the route passing through Flying Monkey Peaks. See *TSL* 39.

119. There is no information on Tao-ch'uan other than that he was in Tung-shan's second generation. *CTL* 17.

120. "Darkling" *(hsüan)* is an important term in the *Lao Tzu*, ch. 1, where it is used to characterize "the named and the nameless," "being and nonbeing," i.e., something prior to dualities. In Buddhist texts it is frequently used to characterize the Path.

121. The identity of Head Monk T'ai is uncertain, but he is possibly Hsüan-t'ai of Nan-yüeh. *TTC* 9.

122. Yu, about whom little is known, is included in *CTL* 17 among numerous other disciples of Tung-shan. He is listed there as Yu-hsi Tao-yu of T'ai-chou.

123. This is the only known record of Shang-tso Lang.

124. Chu-yü of O-chou was a disciple of Nan-ch'üan (748–835) and a member of Ma-tsu's third generation. "Chu-yü" is the name of a mountain on which the *chu-yü,* or oleaster tree, grows.

125. Śramaṇa is a Sanskrit term which literally means "one who exerts himself." In India the term referred to those who, having rejected the authority of received scripture (the *Vedas*), sought to find explanations of the universe and life through their own investigations and reasoning. Most were wanderers who lived by begging. Such seekers first began to appear in India around the 6th or 7th century B.C., and the Buddha himself seems to have been a part of this movement. The term comes to be a general Buddhist designation for one who has renounced home life to practice the Buddhist Way, i.e. a monk or Ho-shang.

126. This approach to practice—that, while training, one should have no consciousness of the process—is found in the *Large Sutra on Perfect Wisdom:* "As by the Lord all dharmas have been pointed out as mere concepts, just so should the Bodhisattva, the great being, having known all *dharmas* as mere concepts, train in perfect wisdom. And why? Because there he does not review the form in which he trains. When he trains thus, the Bodhisattva, the great being, trains in the perfection of giving. And why? Because he does not review the perfection of giving in which he trains." Conze, 1975, p. 215.

127. "Yu-chou is all right, but Hsin-lo is insufferable" was a proverb of the time. Yu-chou was in the extreme north of Hopei, and although still considered part of China, in most ways it was barely distinguishable from the "barbarian" regions north of the border. Hsin-lo, on the other hand, was north of the border and therefore regarded as barbarian and uncivilized. The import seems to be that, although one of two alternatives may be preferable, it is really not much better than the other.

128. "Foot" is used to translate the Chinese term *ch'ih,* a measurement approximating an English foot, and "inch" is used to translate *ts'un,* which is a tenth of a *ch'ih.* Thus, Tung-shan is describing an abnormally long face and short neck.

129. Jan of San-sheng was the monk Hui-jan, a disciple of Lin-chi. San-sheng Temple is in Hopei.

130. Mi of Ching-chao, was a disciple of Kuei-shan (see *TSL* 3) and thus in Ma-tsu's fourth generation. Ching-chao refers to the capital, Ch'ang-an.

131. Hui-chi of Yang-shan (807–883) was Kuei-shan's disciple. Yang Mountain was located in Yuan-chou (Kiangsi).

132. "What is secondary," *ti-erh t'ou,* is a variation of the term translated "secondary views," *ti-erh chien,* in *TSL* 62.

133. In the Ch'in Dynasty, *Shang-shu* was the official title of the "Keeper of the Imperial Archives," coming to designate, by the T'ang, a post comparable to prime minister. The Ch'en here is probably Ch'en-ts'ao, referred to in *CTL* 12 as the governor of Mu-chou. He was a lay disciple of Tao-ts'ung of Mu-chou and thus in Ma-tsu's fifth generation.

134. Reference is being made here to the fifty-two "good friends" or teachers encountered by Sudhana in the *Gaṇḍavyūha* section of the *Avataṃsaka Sūtra.* Each one takes him a step closer to enlightenment. "The stage of subtle consciousness" is the final stage of the fifty-two stages a bodhisattva is said to pass through in order to attain Buddhahood. It is the realization of the Dharma-body.

135. The "end of summer" would be around July 15, since this marks the end of the three-month summer retreat and the beginning of the three-month free period, during which monks often visited other monasteries and teachers.

136. See *TSL* 58.

137. Ch'ing-chu of Shih-shuang (807–888) started in Kuei-shan's congregation but later went to Tao-wu's and eventually became his successor. Thus, he is in Shih-t'ou's fourth generation. Shih-shuang, literally, "rock frost," is the name of a mountain in T'an-chou. *TTC* 6, *CTL* 15.

138. Lists of the "four forms of benevolence" vary, but a popular one, found in the *Ta-ch'eng pen sheng-hsin ti-kuan ching* (T.159), includes the following four: the benevolence appropriate for parents, king, all beings, and the Three Treasures (Buddha, Dharma, Sangha). "The three classes of beings" are the beings existing in the Three Realms of Indian cosmology, i.e., the Realm of Desire, the Realm of Form, and the Formless Realm. According to *The Admonitions of Kuei-shan (Kuei-shan ching-tse),* Buddhists should "constantly strive to repay the kindness of others and rescue beings in the Three Realms."

139. Literally, "beginning and ending."

140. This may be a reference to an incident in the *Avataṃsaka Sūtra* in which Sudhana seeks to visit the first of his fifty-two teachers, Meghaśri (Te-yün), on a mountain peak (see *TSL* 70). But when he arrives, no one is there, Meghaśri having gone to another peak.

141. An account of the "chicken-scaring rhino" is found in the *Teng-she p'ien* of Ko-hung's (284–363) *Pao-p'u tze.* The animal is described as having a red striped horn filled with grain, to which chickens were attracted, only to be frightened away when they got close. The poet Pai Chu-i (772–846) made use of this story in his *Hsin leh fu,* a poem lamenting the death of a rhino presented to

the T'ang emperor Te Tsung. This fabulous animal, native to south Asia, had died in a snow storm en route to the capital.

142. See *TSL* 47.

143. According to the *Śūraṅgama Sūtra* (T.642), ch. 8, and the *Nirvāṇa Sūtra* (T.374), the four mountains are birth, old age, sickness, and death.

144. A "cleared field" would be one from which the old vegetation and remaining seeds have been removed, generally by burning. According to Abhidharma, an *icchantika* is one in whom the "seeds" of spiritual attainment have been so scorched as to destroy their potential.

145. "Pinch" is used to translate the Chinese *liang*, a measure of weight amounting to little more than 30 grams. Incense is normally burned during meditation, and thus this small amount would last only a short time. Tung-shan may be suggesting that the monk has only a short time to live.

146. The Third Patriarch was Seng-ts'an (d. 606). The stupa containing his remains was at Shan-ku Temple in Shu-chou.

147. This is a couplet from a *gāthā* by T'ien-jan of Tan-hsia (738–824), one of Shih-t'ou's leading disciples. Tan-hsia is the name of a peak on which a hermitage was built for T'ien-jan to spend his final years. In the *gāthā*, Tan-hsia claims to have a miraculous jewel which he has kept hidden. Try as they might, others have not been able to discover this jewel. Then, he is "suddenly met by a man who understands emptiness, who has the freedom of these dense woods." (*TTC* 4, 82a,b) This passage is followed by the couplet quoted in the present anecdote.

148. "That which enters through the door is nothing precious" is a quotation from Tung-shan's master, Yün-yen, which appears in *TTC* 5. The following line in that text reads: "Even if your words cause stones to nod their heads, don't value your own affairs."

149. "He is not known by intellect or perceived by consciousness" is from the *Chien ah ch'u Fuo* section of the *Vimalakīrti Nirdeśa Sūtra* (T.14, 555a; Luk, p. 121).

150. "Obtaining the robe and bowl" refers to the well-known story in the first chapter of the *Platform Sutra of the Sixth Patriarch,* according to which Hui-neng rather than Shen-shiu is recognized by the Fifth Patriarch as his successor. This is confirmed by the Fifth Patriarch's entrusting Bodhidharma's robe and bowl to Hui-neng, the underlying assumption being that Hui-neng had attained complete enlightenment. The monk's question concerns the relationship of practice to enlightenment. Shen-hsiu, in his poem written to demonstrate his understanding of Buddhism, says, "Constantly endeavor to wipe it [the mirror] clean." The Fifth Patriarch tells Shen-hsiu that he has only arrived at the door but has not yet entered. Hui-neng's poem includes the line "The bright mirror is originally pure. Where can dust sully it?"

151. "Entering through the door" is the same image used by Tung-shan's teacher, Yün-yen, and quoted by Tung-shan in *TSL* 87: "That which enters through the door is nothing precious." It may also be a further play on Hung-jen's comment that Shen-hsiu had only arrived at the door.

152. "From the beginning not a single thing exists" is a quotation from the *Hsing-yu* section of the the later edition of the *Platform Sutra of the Sixth Patriarch* (Wang Mou-lam, p. 21). It is not found in the earlier Tun-huang edition. Although it is possible that a version different from the Tun-huang edition, containing this line, was in circulation during the ninth century, it is more likely that the use of the line here is an anachronism, indicating that the anecdote was reworked or even composed in the Sung Dynasty.

153. The term "hut-dwelling monk" *(an-chu)* applied to a type of Buddhist monk who led a reclusive existence outside the monastery. According to *CTL* 12, Lin-chi had several such disciples: T'ung-feng *an-chu,* Shan-yang *an-chu,* Hu-chi *an-chu,* and Fu-p'en *an-chu.*

154. Wei-yen of Yüeh-shan (751–834) was Shih-t'ou's disciple and Yün-yen's teacher. Yüeh Mountain was located in Li-chou (Hunan). *TTC* 4, *CTL* 14.

155. "The bird path," an image encountered throughout Buddhist literature, is used to describe the path of an enlightened being. It appears in the Pali *Dhammapada,* 7, as well as in the Perfection of Wisdom literature and its predecessor, the *Ratnaguṇasamucaya Gāthā,* ch. 8, verses 3 and 4: "Having cognized the revolving world as like a snare for wild beasts, the wise roam about similar to the birds in space. He who, coursing perfectly pure, does not course in form or in consciousness, perception, feeling, or will." (Conze, 1973, p. 25) Also in the *Large Sutra on Perfect Wisdom:* "The Lord: Nothing real is meant by the word 'Bodhisattva.' And why? Unproduced is enlightenment, unproduced is a being, and so there is no trace of enlightenment, or of a being [anywhere]. That is why nothing real is meant by the word 'enlightenment-being.' What is meant by the word 'Bodhisattva,' that does not exist, that cannot be apprehended; just as in space, the track of a bird does not exist and cannot be apprehended; . . ." (Conze, 1975, p. 118) See Thomas and J.C. Cleary's translation of a Japanese commentary on the "three paths" taught by Tung-shan in *The Blue Cliff Record,* p. 463.

156. The translation follows the *TTC* 6, in which the character for hemp *(szu)* is used for sandals. The later *WCYL* replaces "hemp" with "self" *(szu),* in which case the sentence might read: "One should go without self underfoot."

157. The image of one's original face appears in the *Hsing-yu* section of the *Platform Sutra of the Sixth Patriarch.* See note 89.

158. The *WCYL* appends the following anecdote:

> Later a monk at Chia-shan's (805–881) assembly was asked, "Where did you come from?"
>
> "From Tung-shan's," replied the monk.
>
> "What does Tung-shan teach his followers?" asked Chia-shan.
>
> "He ordinarily teaches his students three ways," said the monk.
>
> "What are those three ways?" asked Chia-shan.
>
> "The darkling way *(hsüan lu),* the bird path, and the open hand *(chan shou),*" replied the monk.
>
> "Does he really have these teachings?" asked Chia-shan.

"Yes," replied the monk.

"Notes resolutely grasped for one thousand *li*, the sorrow of the students of the Way in the Monk's Hall," said Chia-shan.

159. "Amidst the darkling, darken again" is a variation on a line from the first chapter of the *Tao-te-ching*, "Darken it and darken again."

160. Vairocana is found throughout the *Avataṃsaka Sūtra*, T.278, and the *Brahmajāla Sūtra*, T.1484, where he appears as the ruling Buddha of the Lotuswomb Realm. He represents the most metaphysically elevated Buddha of the Mahāyāna tradition, capable of manifesting himself as all the other Buddhas.

161. "Multitudinous things" appears to refer to conditioned things *(saṃskṛta dharma)*, i.e., the phenomenal world, and raises the question of how something unconditioned *(asaṃskṛita)*, i.e., the Buddha, can exist in the world.

162. The "once" in the present text *(WCYL)* replaces "always" in the earlier *TTS*. Thus the line might also read, "I am always very concerned about that."

163. The four lines Tung-shan is asked to comment on are a *gāthā* by Lungshan that appears in *TTC* 20 where it is part of the same encounter described in *TSL* 23.

164. T'ung Pass is a major pass between Ch'ang-an, the imperial capital, and Lo-yang. It was regarded as the entrance to Ch'ang-an.

165. The following anecdote is appended to this one:

> Later a monk asked Ts'ao-shan, "What does 'one is old' mean?"
> "No support," replied Ts'ao-shan.
> "What does 'one is not old' mean?" asked the monk.
> "A withered, dead tree," answered Ta'so-shan.

166. Wu-hsieh was one of Tung-shan's early teachers (see *TSL* 1). Although he is said here to have attained enlightenment under Shih-t'ou, he eventually entered Ma-tsu's lineage.

167. Ten feet, a foot, and an inch do not correspond exactly to the *chang, ch'ih,* and *ts'un* of the Chinese text. A *chang* contains ten *ch'ih,* and a *ch'ih* ten *ts'un.* A *ts'un* is slightly more than an inch.

168. Tung-t'ing Lake, China's largest lake, is located in northern Hunan.

169. This *gāthā* borrows the form of *Wu keng chuan*, a folk song popular in the ninth century. *Wei* has generally been translated "rank," (See Heinrich Dumoulin, 1953, p. 25.) However, since the five do not have any clearly ascending order, the term can be understood in a more neutral sense, such as "mode" or "position." "Lord and vassal," an image for the Real and phenomena, is part of the title of Tung-shan's poetic rendering of the Five Ranks doctrine. See *TSL* 115.

170. The night is divided into five two-hour watches *(keng)*, running from 8 *p.m.* to 6 *a.m.* Therefore, the third watch would begin at midnight.

171. Instead of "familiar" *(yen)*, the *WCYL* reads "dispised" *(hsien)*. This reading, however, appears to be a misprint, since not only does it conflict with

the rhyme scheme, but it is also not supported by a quotation of this line in the *Record of Ts'ao-shan* (T.14, 550b). This latter text confirms the present reading of "familiar."

172. The "lotus amidst fire" is an image in the *Vimalakīrti Nirdeśa Sūtra* representing the bodhisattva's vow to practice meditation in the midst of desires. (T.14, 550b; Luk, p.90)

173. The *ch'i lin* is a mythological beast, with the characteristics of a dragon, a deer, and the Greek Pegasus. It is traditionally regarded as the mount of sylphs.

174. In *TTC* 16, Nan-ch'üan asks Tao-wu, "What can you say about that place that knowledge does not reach?" Tao-wu replied, "One should absolutely avoid talking about that." Nan-ch'üan said, "Truly, as soon as one explains, horns sprout on one's head, and one becomes a beast."

175. See *TSL* 53.

176. The "fifty-three" is a reference to Sudhana's fifty-three teachers in the *Gaṇḍavyūha* section of the *Avataṃsaka Sūtra*, T.278. These are the same as the "fifty-two" in *TSL* 70 and 76. Although only fifty-two different teachers were visited by Sudhana, one of the bodhisattvas is visited twice (the first and last encounters). Therefore, the number is sometimes given as fifty-three.

177. Pen-chi of Ts'ao-shan (840–901), one of Tung-shan's eight principal disciples, had been a student of Confucius before becoming a monk at the age of nineteen. He didn't meet Tung-shan until much later in his life. Probably best known for his commentaries on Tung-shan's doctrine of the "five ranks." He eventually established his own center on Ts'ao Mountain in Hung-chou (Kiangsi). Although Ts'ao-shan's line died out almost immediately, his comments on this doctrine survived and have had a major influence on Ch'an and on Far Eastern culture in general. This anecdote is his only actual appearance in the *TSL*, though his name is mentioned in Tung-shan's memorial (*TSL* 120). *CTL* 15.

178. The "jewel mirror" is an image that appears frequently in Buddhist literature; it can be found, for example, in the *Ta-chih-tu lun*, ch. 6, and the *Vimalakīrti Nirdeśa Sūtra*.

179. This simile is found throughout the *Ta-chih-tu lun*, e.g. "Perfect wisdom is like a great ball of flame; it can't be grasped from any side." *Ta-chih-tu lun*, ch. 19; T.25, 190c.

180. In ch. 20, *Ying-erh hsing* section of the *Nirvāṇa Sūtra*, (T.12, 728–29), the "five characteristics" of the common infant are explained as analogous to the behavior of the *Tathāgata*, i.e., an infant is characterized by the inability to get up, stay put, come, go away, or talk. Similarly, the *Tathāgata* does not "raise" the thought of any dharma; does not "abide" in any dharma; does not have a body that would be capable of action (such as "coming"); does not "go" anywhere because he is already in nirvana, and, although he has taught the Dharma for living beings, has in fact "said" nothing. Also, according to this analogy, the infant is described as producing the sounds *p'uo ho* (seemingly meaningless sounds, translated here as *ba* and *wa*), where *p'uo* is equated with the *Tathāgata's* teaching of permanence and the unconditioned, and *ho* with the teaching of imperma-

nence and the conditioned. Thus, "speaking without speaking" describes this latter characteristic of teaching without recourse to intelligible speech. It also seems possible to interpret this to imply that what is generally accepted as intelligible speech and does in fact concern the conditioned and unconditioned—e.g., the sutras—is no more than the incoherent sounds of an infant when compared to ultimate reality.

181. This and the previous line develop the idea of the Five Ranks in terms of five hexagrams from the *Book of Changes (I Ching)*. Partially because of the ambiguity of exactly how the five transformations are to be performed, opinions have varied on what the five configurations are. A considerable body of commentary exists, beginning with Ts'ao-shan and continuing up to the present time. (See Alfonso Verdu, 1966). Yanagida suggests the following five configurations and the "ranks" to which each corresponds: (1) "Phenomena within the Real" is the double *sun* hexagram; (2) "the Real within phenomena" is the double *tui;* (3) "coming from within the Real" is *tui* above, *sun* below; (4) "going within together" is *sun* above, *tui* below; and (5) "arriving within together" is the double *li* (Yanagida,1974, p. 383). A description of these hexagrams can be found in Baynes and Wilhelm's translation of the *I Ching*, 1950.

182. The *vajra,* or "thunderbolt," is a ritual device often held while teaching. There are various numbers of prongs on the ends of a *vajra,* one, three, or five being most common. The one referred to here is clearly a five-pronged *vajra.*

183. In the discussion of the trigram *li* in the *I Ching* there appears the following comment: "Nine at the beginning. Treading with circumspection; if one acts with respect, there is no blame."

184. This is not the traditional Buddha, Shakyamuni, but the Buddha Mahābhijñānābhibhu (the Buddha of Supreme Penetration and Surpassing Wisdom). According to the *Hua ch'eng yu* section of the *Avataṃsaka Sūtra,* he is said to have spent ten kalpas in meditation before attaining Buddhahood. His prolonged meditation became a popular topic in Ch'an literature. See *The Gateless Gate (Wu men kuan),* case 9, and *The Record of Lin-chi* (Sasaki, p. 32).

185. In popular lore the tiger is noted for eating all of its prey but the ears. The significance of this as well as of the whitened left hind leg of a charger is not entirely clear, but Yanagida suggests that they are indicative of venerability and power, the tiger as the master of the mountain beasts and the spirited horse as one whose hind leg has whitened with age. Yanagida, 1974, pp. 383–84.

186. The "jeweled footrest and brocade robes" alludes to the story in the *Hsin chieh* ("Faith Discernment") chapter of the *Lotus Sutra* (Kato pp. 111–25), in which a prodigal son, who had run away from home and wandered about for many years, finally returns home and, seeing his father dressed in brocade robes, feet resting on a jeweled footrest, does not recognize him. The father employs his son in menial tasks, for which the son is very grateful, never suspecting the true wealth to which he is heir. As the father is dying, the secret is finally revealed to the son. This is expained in the chapter as similar to the ignorance of those who are content with progress toward nirvana, never realizing their true potential as "sons of the Buddha."

187. Nan-ch'üan (see *TSL* 2) is recorded as saying in *TTS* 16, 297a, "It is frequently said, 'Patriarchs and Buddhas do not know reality. Wildcats and white oxen do.'" The passage goes on to explain that this is because in these animals there is not the least discrimination.

188. Yi is noted in traditional Chinese mythology as the skilled archer, who, at the command of the legendary Yao (2357–2257 B.C.), shot nine of the ten suns from the sky in order to save the crops.

189. This refers to an unnamed archer in the *Chou pen chi* section of the *Shih chi (Recors of the Historian)* who was able to pierce a willow leaf at 100 paces.

190. "Two arrow points meeting head-on" was a popular image that has its origin in the *T'ang wen* chapter of the *Lieh-tzu*. A famous archer named Fei-wei taught his technique to his student, Chi-ch'ang. Chi-ch'ang decided that, were he to kill his teacher, no one could compete with him. However, in attempting this, he unknowingly failed. When later the two met on a small country road, Chi-ch'ang shot at Fei-wei, who in turn shot his own arrow. The two arrows met in mid-flight and fell harmlessly to the ground. As a result, Chi-ch'ang was enlightened to his own selfishness and developed a more profound relationship with his teacher. Shih-t'ou also uses this image in his poem *Ts'an t'ung ch'i:* "In the case of phenomena, the lid must fit the box; compliance with principle is like arrowheads meeting head-on." *TTS*4, 77b.) See T. Cleary, 1980, p.37.

191. "Perfect rest," meaning nirvana, is a euphemism for death.

192. *Wu-pen* is literally "root of awakening."

193. The location of this mountain has long been uncertain, but it is probably somewhere in the vicinity of Tung Mountain.

194. Yu-chang hsien is in present-day central Kiangsi province.

195. The "three root types" is a traditional Buddhist categorization of people according to their capacity for religious understanding set forth in the second chapter of the *Abhidharmakośa Śāstra* of Vasubandhu. In the first category are those who see but do not yet comprehend the Dharma. In the second are those in the process of attaining an understanding. And in the third are those who have already understood. Thus, Tung-shan is credited with the ability to instruct all seekers, regardless of their inherent capacity. Lin-chi makes a similar claim with regard to people of the "three kinds of root capacity" and labels the categories "below average," "above average," and "superior." T.47, 501b; Sasaki, p. 29.

196. According to the *Vimalakīrti Nirdeśa Sūtra* (T.14, 538a) the Buddha is said to utter only a single sound, which is variously interpreted depending on the listener's capacity to understand. "The Buddha expounds the Dharma with a single sound. People understand variously, each according to their type."

197. "Jewel" *(pao)* is often prefixed to Buddhist and Taoist terms. In addition to being prefixed to "sword" in this text, it is also prefixed to "mirror" in *TSL* 117, the "Jewel Mirror *Samādhi.*" Both are implements serving a spiritual end. Bodhisattvas and guardian deities are often described as holding such swords for the purpose of cutting off defilements; e.g., Mañjuśrī is iconographically represented as holding a sword, said to be for cutting off ignorance.

198. There are two explanations concerning the name of the lineage. In one, *Ts'ao-tung* is regarded as a combination of the names of Tung-shan and his disciple Ts'ao-shan. However, according to adherents of the line of another of Tung-shan's disciples, Yün-chü, *ts'ao* refers to the name of the Sixth Patriarch's center, Ts'ao-hsi.

Index of Figures Mentioned
in The Record of Tung-shan
(* Disciples of Tung-shan)

Bibliography

A. Works in the Buddhist Canon

A-pi-ta-mo chü-she lun. (Abhidharmakośa Śāstra.) Vasubandhu. T.29 (no. 1558), pp. 1–161.

Abhdiharmakośa Śāstra. See *A-pi-to-mo chü-she lun.*

A-mi-t'o ching. (Sukhāvatīvyūha Sūtra). T.12 (no. 366), pp. 346–48.

Aṣṭasāhasrikā Prajñāpāramitā Sūtra. See *Pa-ch'ien sung pan-jo-po-lo-mi-to ching.*

Avataṃsaka Sūtra. See *Ta-fang-kuang fuo hua-yen ching.*

Blue Cliff Record. See *Pi-yen lu.*

Brahmajāla Sūtra. See *Fan-wang ching.*

Chen-chou Lin-chi Hui-chao ch'an-shih yü-lu. Hui-jan. T.47 (no. 1985), pp. 495–506. Translated by Ruth Fuller Sasaki, *The Record of Lin-chi,* Kyoto: The Institute for Zen Studies, 1975.

Chin-kang pan-jo-po-lo-mi ching. (Vajracchedikā Prajñāpāramitā Sūtra.) T.8 (no. 235), pp. 748–52. *The Diamond Sutra.* Translated from Sanskrit by Edward Conze in the *Buddhist Wisdom Books,* New York: Harper and Row, 1958.

Ching-te ch'uan-teng lu. Tao-yüan. T.51 (no. 2076), pp. 196–469. *The Ching-te Record of the Transmissions of the Lamp.* Partial translation by Chang Chung-yuan in *Original Teachings of Ch'an Buddhism,* New York: Vintage Books, 1971.

Ch'uan fa-pao chi. Tu-fei. T.85 (no. 2838), pp. 1291.

Dhammapada. Translated by Juan Mascaro, *The Dhammapada,* Baltimore, Md.: Penguin, 1973.

Diamond Sutra. See *Chin-kang pan-jo-po-lo-mi ching.*

Fan-wang ching. (Brahmajāla Sūtra.) T.24 (no. 1484), pp. 997–1010.

Fuo-mu pao-te-tsang pan-jo-po-lo-mi-tuo ching. (Ratnaguṇasamucaya Gāthā.) T.8 (no. 229), pp. 676–84. Translated by Edward Conze in *The Perfection of Wisdom in Eight Thousand Lines and Its Verse Summary,* Bolinas, Calif.: Four Seasons Foundation, 1973.

Heart Sutra. See *Pan-jo-po-lo-mi-tuo hsin ching.*

Hsin hsin ming. (Inscription on Believing in Mind.) Seng-ts'an. T.48 (no. 2010), pp. 376–77. Translated by D. T. Suzuki in *Manual of Zen Buddhism,* New York: Grove Press, 1960, pp. 76–82.

Hsü kao-seng chuan. Tao-hsüan. T.50 (no. 2060), pp. 425–707.
Hua-yen k'ung mu chang. Chih-yen. T.45 (no. 1870), pp. 536–89.
Inscription on Believing in Mind. See *Hsin hsin ming.*
Jui-chou Tung-shan Liang-chieh ch'an-shih yü-lu. Yü-feng Yüan-hsin. T.47 (no.
    1986B), pp. 519–26. *The Record of Tung-shan Liang-chieh of Jui-chou.*
    There are two Japanese translations: Horyu Sahashi, "Tōzan roku" *Zen no
    koten, chugoku,* ed. Keiji Nishitani. Tokyo: Chikuma Shōbo, 1968; Seizan
    Yanagida in *Zen goroku, Seikai no meicho, 3.* Tokyo: Chuo Koron sha,
    1974.
Kao-seng chuan. Hui-chiao. T.50 (no. 2059), pp. 322–425.
Laṅkāvatāra Sūtra. See *Leng-chia-a-p'o-to-lo pao ching.*
Large Sutra on Perfect Wisdom. See *Mo-ho-pan-jo-po-lo-mi ching.*
Leng-chia-a-p'o-to-lo pao ching. (Laṅkāvatāra Sūtra.) T.16 (no. 670), pp. 479–
    514. Translated by D. T. Suzuki, *The Lankavatara Sutra,* London: Rout-
    ledge & Kegan Paul, 1956.
Li-tai fa-pao chi. T.51 (no. 2075), pp. 179–96.
Lotus Sutra. See *Miao-fa lien-hua ching.*
Maitreya Sūtra. See *Mi-le hsia-sheng ching.*
Mi-le hsia-sheng ching. T.14 (no. 454), pp. 423–26.
Miao-fa lien-hua ching. (Saddharmapuṇḍarīka Sūtra.) T.9 (no. 262), pp. 1–61.
    Translated by Bunno Kato, Yoshiro Tamura, and Kojiro Miyasaka, *The
    Threefold Lotus Sutra,* New York: Weatherhill, 1975.
Mo-ho-pan-jo-po-lo-mi ching. (Pañcaviṃśatisāhasrikā Prajñāpāramitā Sūtra.)
    T.8 (no. 223), pp. 217–425. A later version of the Sanskrit text has been
    translated by Edward Conze, *The Large Sutra on Perfect Wisdom,* Berkeley:
    University of California Press, 1975.
*Nan-tsung tun-chiao tsui-shang ta-ch'eng mo-ho-pan-jo-po-lo-mi ching: Liu-tsu
    Hui-neng ta-shih yü Shao-chou Ta-fan ssu shih-fa t'an ching.* T.48 (no.
    2007), pp. 337–45. This version, which is the earliest, has been translated
    by Philip Yampolski, *The Platform Sutra of the Sixth Patriarch,* New York:
    Columbia University Press, 1967. *Liu-tsu ta-shih fa-pao t'an ching.* T.48
    (no. 2008), pp. 345–65, is the later Sung edition and has been translated by
    Wong Mou-lam in *The Diamond Sutra and the Sutra of Hui Neng,* Boulder,
    Colo.: Shambhala, 1984.
Nirvāṇa Sūtra. See *Ta-pan nieh-p'an ching.*
Pan-jo-po-lo-mi-tuo hsin ching. (Prajñāpāramitā Hṛdaya Sūtra) T.8 (no. 251),
    pp. 848–49. *The Heart Sutra.* Translated by Edward Conze in *The Buddhist
    Wisdom Books,* New York: Harper & Row, 1958.
Pa-ch'ien sung pan-jo-po-lo-mi-tuo ching. (Aṣṭasāhasrikā Prajñāpāramitā Sūtra.)
    T.6 (no. 224), pp. 425–78. Translated by Edward Conze in *The Perfection
    of Wisdom in Eight Thousand Lines and Its Verse Summary,* Bolinas, Calif.:
    Four Seasons Foundation, 1973.
Perfection of Wisdom in Eight Thousand Lines. See *Pa-ch'ien sung pan-jo-po-lo-
    mi-tuo ching.*
Pi-yen lu. Yüan-wu K'o-ch'in. T.48 (no. 2003), pp. 139–225. Translated by Tho-

mas and J. C. Cleary, *The Blue Cliff Record,* Boulder, Colo.: Shambhala, 1977.

Platform Sutra of the Sixth Patriarch. See *Nan-tsung tun-chiao tsui-shang ta-ch'eng mo-ho-pan-jo-po-lo-mi ching: Liu-tsu Hui-neng ta-shih yü Shao-chou Ta-fan ssu shih-fa t'an ching.*

Ratnaguṇasamucaya Gāthā. See *Fuo-mu pao-te-tsang pan-jo-po-lo-mi-tuo ching.*

Record of Lin-chi. See *Chen-chou Lin-chi Hui-chao ch'an-shih yü-lu.*

Saddharmapuṇḍarīka Sūtra. See *Miao-fa lien-hua ching.*

Shou-leng-yen ching. T.15 (no. 642), pp. 629–45. Translated by Charles Luk, *The Surangama Sutra,* London: Rider, 1966.

Ssu-fen lü. T.22 (no. 1428), pp. 567–1015.

Sukhāvatīvyūha Sūtra. See *A-mi-t'o ching.*

Sung kao-seng chuan. Tsan-ning. T.50 (no. 2061), pp. 709–900.

Śūraṅgama Sūtra. See *Shou-leng-yen ching.*

Ta-ch'eng pen sheng-hsin ti-kuan ching. T.3 (no. 159), pp.291–331.

Ta-chih-tu lun. T.25 (no. 1509), pp. 57–758.

Ta-fang-kuang-fuo hua-yen ching. (60 *chuan* version, *Avataṃsaka Sūtra.*) T.9 (no. 278), pp. 395. Partially translated by Thomas Cleary, *The Flower Ornament Scripture,* vol. 1, Boulder, Colo.: Shambhala, 1984.

Ta-pan nieh-p'an ching. (Mahānirvāṇa Sūtra.) T.12 (no. 374), pp. 365–605; T.12 (no. 375), pp. 605–853.

Tōzan Gohon zenji goroku. Gimoku Genkai. T.57 (no. 1986A), pp. 507–19.

Tsa pi-yu ching. Tao-lueh. T.4 (no. 207), pp. 522–31.

Ts'ung-jung lu. T.48 (no. 2004), pp. 226–92.

Tsu-men ching-hsun. Ju-chin. T.48 (no. 2023), pp. 1040–97.

Vajracchedikā Prajñāpāramitā Sūtra. See *Chin-kang pan-jo-po-lo-mi ching.*

Vimalakīrti Nirdeśa Sūtra. See *Wei-mo chieh-suo-shuo ching.*

Wei-mo chieh-suo-shuo ching. (Vimalakīrti Nirdeśa Sūtra.) T.14 (no. 475), pp. 537–57. Translated by Charles Luk, *The Vimalakirti Nirdesa Sutra,* Boulder, Colo.: Shambhala, 1972.

Wu-men kuan. Tsung-shao. T.48 (no. 2005), pp. 292–300. *The Gateless Gate.* Translated by Katsuki Sekida in *Two Zen Classics: Mumonkan and Hekiganroku,* New York: Weatherhill, 1977.

B. Pre-modern Works

Analects of Confucius. See *Lun yü.*

Ch'an-men chu-tsu-shih chi-sung. Z.2, 21,5.

Ch'an-tsung cheng-mai. Ju-chin. Z.2, 19, 1–2.

Ch'an-yüan ch'ing-kuei. Ch'ang-lu Tsung-che.

Chuang-tzu. Translated by Burton Watson, *The Complete Works of Chuang Tzu,* New York: Columbia University Press, 1968.

Fa-yün chih-lüeh. Chih-p'an. Nanking. 1936. Translated by Jan, Yün-hua, *A Chronicle of Buddhism in China, 581–960 A.D.,* Calcutta: Visva-Bharati, 1966.

Ganjin kakai daishi tō sei den.
Hasshu ko yo. Gyozen. *Dai-Nihon Bukkyo Zensho,* III. 1913.
Hsü ku-tsun hsu yü-yao. Z.2, 23, 5–24, 1.
I Ching. Translation by Cary F. Baynes of Richard Wilhelm's German version, *The I Ching or Book of Changes.* New York: Pantheon Books. 1950.
Kuei-shan ching-tse. Ling-yu.
Lieh-tzu.
Lun-yü. Translated by Arthur Waley, *The Analects of Confucius,* New York: Random House, 1938.
Meng-tzu. Translated by D. C. Lau, *Mencius,* New York: Penguin, 1970.
Nan-yang ho-shang tun-chiao chieh-t'o ch'an-men chih-liao-hsing t'an yü. Pelliot 2045 (2).
Pao-lin chuan.
Pao-p'u tze. The "inner chapters" *(nei p'ien)* have been translated by James Ware, *Alchemy, Medicine and Religion in the China of* A.D. *320,* New York: Dover Publications, 1966.
Shen-hui ho-shang i-chi. Hu Shih. Shanghai, 1930.
Shih-chi. Translated by Burton Watson, *Records of the Grand Historian of China: Translated from the Shih Chi of Ssu-ma Ch'ien,* 2 vols., New York: Columbia University Press, 1961.
Sōtō ni shi roku. Shigetsu Ein.
Tao te ching. Translated by D. C. Lau, *Lao Tzu: Tao Te Ching,* New York: Penguin, 1963.
Ts'ao-hsi ta-shih pieh chuan.
Tsu-t'ang chi. Kyoto, 1974.
Tsung-men shih-kuei lun. Z.2, 15, 5.
Wu-chia yü-lu. Kyoto, 1974.
Yüan-chueh ching ta shu-ch'ao. Tsung-mi. Z.1, 14, 3–5.

C. Recent Studies and Secondary Works

Bielefeldt, Carl and Lewis Lancaster
   1975   *"T'an Ching* (Platform Scripture)," *Philosophy East and West,* 25, no. 2, 1975. pp. 197–212.

Cleary, Thomas
   1978   *Sayings and Doings of Pai-chang.* Los Angeles: Center Publications. 1978.
   1980   *Timeless Spring.* Tokyo: Weatherhill.

Demiéville, Paul
   1970   "Le Recueil de la Salle des Patriarches *'Tsou-t'ang tsi,'* " *T'oung Pao,* 56, pp. 262–86.
   1973   Choix d'etudes sinologiques. Leiden, Netherlands: E. J. Brill.

Dumoulin, Heinrich
1953   *The Development of Chinese Zen After the Sixth Patriarch.* New York: First Zen Institute.
1963   *A History of Zen Buddhism.* Boston: Beacon Press.
1979   *Zen Enlightement.* Trans. John Maraldo. New York: Weatherhill.

Lai, Whalen
1979   "Ch'an Metaphors: Waves, Water, Mirror, Lamp," *Philosophy East and West,* Vol. 29, no. 3.

McRae, John
1983   "The Oxhead School of Chinese Ch'an Buddhism: From Early Ch'an to the Golden Age," *Studies in Ch'an and Hua-yen,* ed. Robert M. Gimello and Peter N. Gregory. Honolulu, Hawaii: University of Hawaii Press.
1986   *The Northern School and the Formation of Early Ch'an Buddhism.* Honolulu, Hawaii: University of Hawaii Press.

Ui, Hakuju
1943   *Zenshu shi kenkyū,* vols. 1–3. Tokyo: Iwanami Shoten.

Verdu, Alfonso
1966   "The 'Five Ranks' Dialectic," *Monumenta Niponica,* 21, nos. 1–2, 1966.

Yampolski, Philip
1982   "New Japanese Studies in Early Ch'an History," *Early Ch'an in Tibet and China,* ed. Whalen Lai and Lewis Lancaster. Berkeley, Calif.: Lancaster-Miller.

Yanagida, Seizan
1967   *Shoki zenshu shisho no kenkyū.* Tokyo: Hozokan.
1968   *Rinzai no kafu.* Tokyo: Chikuma Shobo.
1969   "Zenshu goroku no keisei," *Indo gaku bukkyō gaku kenkyū,* 18, no. 1. 1969. Translated by John McRae, "The 'Recorded Sayings' Texts of Chinese Ch'an Buddhism," in *Early Ch'an in China and Tibet,* ed. Whalen Lai and Lewis Lancaster. Berkeley: Lancaster-Miller, 1982.
1970   *Mu no tankyū.* Tokyo: Kadokawa Shoten.
1976   *Shoki no zenshi II: Rekidai hōbō ki, II —, Zen no goroku,* 3. Tokyo: Chikuma Shōbo.

Production Notes

This book was designed by Roger Eggers.
Composition and paging were done on the
Quadex Composing System and typesetting on
the Compugraphic 8400 by the design and
production staff of University of Hawaii Press.

The text and display typeface is Sabon.

Offset presswork and binding were done by
Malloy Lithographing, Inc. Text paper is Glat-
felter Offset Vellum, basis 50.